Collecting American Belleek

Loman & Petula Eng

Schiffer Publishing Ltd®

4880 Lower Valley Road, Atglen, PA 19310 USA

Dedication

To our daughter, son, and mothers with love.

The current values provided in this guide are intended as references and not to set prices for readers. Values vary from time to time and are affected by condition as well as demand. Neither the authors nor the publisher assumes responsibility for any losses that might be incurred as a result of using this book as a reference.

Designed by Mark David Bowyer
Type set in Zapf Chancery Bd BT/Korinna BT

ISBN: 0-7643-1860-8
Printed in China
1 2 3 4

Published by Schiffer Publishing Ltd.
4880 Lower Valley Road
Atglen, PA 19310
Phone: (610) 593-1777; Fax: (610) 593-2002
E-mail: Info@schifferbooks.com
Please visit our web site catalog at **www.schifferbooks.com**
We are always looking for people to write books on new and related subjects. If you have an idea for a book please contact us at the above address.

This book may be purchased from the publisher.
Include $3.95 for shipping.
Please try your bookstore first.
You may write for a free catalog.

In Europe, Schiffer books are distributed by
Bushwood Books
6 Marksbury Ave.
Kew Gardens
Surrey TW9 4JF England
Phone: 44 (0)20-8392-8585
Fax: 44 (0)20-8392-9876
E-mail: Bushwd@aol.com
Free postage in the UK. Europe: air mail at cost

Contents

Acknowledgments

This book took us about two years to prepare and write. It would not have been possible without the help and insights of many friends, fellow dealers, collectors, and, most importantly, our children, Vicky and Victor, who edited the manuscript.

We thank our publisher, Peter Schiffer, of Schiffer Publishing, Ltd. for providing us the opportunity to publish this book in full colors, and his staff for all of the help they gave us during the production period.

We are especially grateful to Jeff Snyder for his time and expertise in helping us overcome many technical issues during our preparation of this book, especially the photographs. We also thank Wendy M. Nardi, Historian and Curator of Trentoniana at the Trenton Public Library in Trenton, New Jersey, and Stephanie Morgano of Ellarslie, The Trenton City Museum, for their effort in helping us find much information about American Belleek.

While it is not possible to mention all of our friends by name, who gave us direct support and encouragement in the last two years, we would like to express our appreciation to them for helping us find the references and dated materials. Thank you.

Preface

American art ceramics made in the late 1800s to early 1900s represent a very important part of our nation's art history. As a nation of immigrants, our country flourishes with the collective talent of people from around the world. This is just as true in art as in technology and other areas. Although many artists came from abroad with their skills, many Americans went overseas to learn the skills before returning to the country. There were also many talented artists who developed their skills here in America. The result was the pinnacle in craftsmanship shown by the best of both worlds.

There is a misconception that art ceramics made by Americans in the nineteenth century and early twentieth century are inferior to those made overseas. If you take American art pottery vases, such as Grueby or Rookwood vases, and compare them to vases made in Europe, they are just as good, if not better. If you take a Ceramic Art Company (CAC) vase, hand-painted with a female portrait by H. J. Nosek, and compare it to a Nippon transfer-print female portrait vase (most Nippon portrait items were print-transferred and mass produced), the American vase is far superior to the Japanese one. So why is it that the Nippon vase is valued higher than the American vase? If you put a William Morley plate decorated with orchids next to *any* Limoges plate decorated with flowers, the American plate is not inferior to the French one. So why should the Morley plate be sold for less? If, in the world of antiques, with all other things being equal, a rarer piece commands a higher price, then, in fact, American art porcelain should be valued much more because they are much scarcer. Production of American Belleek in particular lasted only a very short period of about fifty years. In fact, one of the best companies in this field, Ott & Brewer, lasted for only ten years.

This book is not trying to compare art ceramics made in America with those made overseas. Both have their own merits and are collectible. This book is trying to bring to the attention of fellow American collectors that there is a neglected treasure right at home. We hope that it will generate more interest among collectors of American art ceramics, especially American Belleek made from the late 1800s to early 1900s, or even mid-1900s. They are part of our cultural heritage. Today, almost all of the porcelain wares that we use are made overseas. We do not foresee any possibility of the revival of this industry in America in the coming future. Therefore, as Mary Gaston said, "Porcelain made during the American Belleek Era is truly an exciting field of collecting."

Although we have a few examples of Lenox pieces made after 1930, this book focuses mainly on the discussion of three companies, Ceramic Art Company-Lenox pre-1930, Willets, and Ott & Brewer, because they represent the three most important companies of that era. Also, their porcelains are more readily available in the market than others, which provide us with a larger database/sample size in order to evaluate their items. For those companies whose products are hard to come by, opinion can hardly be formed to warrant in-depth discussion on them. Therefore, we do not want to discuss them and their items separately. Instead, we will group them together at the end of this book and show a few pieces of the items made by those companies as illustrations. The values we provide for these items are based on more subjective opinions provided by a few dealers rather than by a larger database and a more objective evaluation. In other words, their values depend on how much an individual collector is willing to pay for them. Finally, although Knowles, Taylor & Knowles China Company was a very good company, their production period of American Belleek was about two years from 1887-1889. When KTK reopened its business around 1891, after the fire that destroyed its factory in 1889, the products made by them were not called "Belleek." Also, the clay composition was more like bone china than that of Irish Belleek (Barber, 1893). Thus we consider most of their products as American art porcelain and do not include them under a separate topic in this book. Their famous Lotus Ware is a category of its own, and we include a few items of it in this book.

We have included a few pieces of "modern" Lenox porcelain that were made after 1950 for several reasons. First, a few of these pieces were decorated by renowned artists, such as a rose vase by H. J. Nosek in the early 1950s with a gold wreath mark (Plate 11) or another rose vase by George Morley after 1932 with a green wreath mark (with "Made in USA" mark, Plate 16.) The second reason is that there are many undecorated (white) porcelain pieces that are so artistically designed. They represent a short but important history of modern porcelain, and we would like to share them with our readers. Thus, we showed a few vases (Plates 175 to 178) that express their beauty without the distraction of colors in this book, although they were made after the 1960s. The third reason is that there are numerous Lenox items that were made with the "Made in USA" mark which are worth collecting. They were either made from the old designs before 1930 or in their own new appearance after 1930. Finally, we include a few new pieces to show examples with different gold marks.

No matter how careful we were and how much effort we put into this book, we realize that there may be some errors. We sincerely welcome suggestions and corrections and shall incorporate them in our future revision(s) or book(s). Also, no matter how hard we attempt to be as objective as possible, many of the opinions we discuss in this book are based on our own experiences, and not everyone will agree with them, for everyone has his or her own personal experiences. Finally, except for the history of the companies, we are going to present this book in a more casual fashion than most other books. In other words, we are going to *chat* with you, as if we were chatting in your living room. After all, collecting American Belleek should be more for pleasure than academic research. Enjoy it.

Chapter 1
A Brief History of American Belleek

When you mention the word Belleek to someone who is familiar with antique porcelain, the first thing that comes to his or her mind would be the Irish Belleek, the delicate eggshell-like porcelain with a nacreous lustre of various tints. The nacreous lustre was invented by a French chemist name Brianchon around 1857. The thin porcelain body was invented by William H. Goss of Stoke-on-Trent, England, probably around the same time. It was made from feldspathic clays and salts of bismuth colored with metallic oxides. Like hard paste porcelain it is translucent and vitreous; but unlike hard paste porcelain, it achieves both qualities only after one firing. It is called "parian" after the first firing. On the other hand, the hard paste porcelain is called "bisque" after the first firing and it becomes translucent but not vitreous. Only after glaze firing would the bisque body vitrify because the glaze melts into the body. The glaze firing on a parian body only gives it an overlay effect without having the glaze melt into the body. In 1851 a stratum of feldspathic clay was found in the village of Belleek, County of Fermanagh, Ireland. David McBirney and Robert William Armstrong saw the opportunity and built a pottery there in 1857. They enticed William Bromley Sr., Goss's manager, to help them with the technique of making Belleek wares. Eventually, William Bromley Sr. was responsible for spreading the techniques from Stoke-on Trent to Ireland, and then to the United States. By 1872 McBirney and Armstrong proudly presented their Belleek wares at the Dublin Exposition. After Queen Victoria became one of their many famous customers, Irish Belleek quickly became the pride of the Irish potters and envy of potters from America.

About the time when McBirney and Armstrong established their pottery in Ireland, the City of Trenton, New Jersey, in the eastern United States, began to emerge as the premier pottery producing center. In that region, natural resources played a role, too. The Raritan Formation of New Jersey's Inner Coastal Plain contains thick Late Cretaceous clay beds laid down some 70 to 100 million years ago in a marine environment. These clays are excellent for making pottery. Trenton also has a geographical advantage because it is located midway between the major markets of New York City and Philadelphia. The Delaware and Raritan Canal connect it directly to both cities. The Delaware Canal and the Belvidere-Delaware Railroad brought coal from Pennsylvania to fuel the kilns while the Camden & Amboy railroad and the Delaware & Bound Brook Railroad brought other raw materials needed for the pottery. Finished goods could be quickly distributed to the markets through these same routes as well. In addition, with the availability of capital and industrial labor, the encouragement of government, and the easy acceptance of industrialized culture in the region, Trenton became a manufacturing center of iron, steel, textile, rubber, and pottery making (Potteries of Trenton Society). In 1852, only one potter, McCully, operated in that area with one kiln. By 1868, fifteen major potteries with about fifty kilns and sales close to half a million were making products there. In 1883, the area had twenty-three potteries with 110 kilns and sales close to $2.7 million. Around 1900, Trenton had about forty-one potteries operating 258 kilns. Total pottery production exceeded $5.5 million, which was estimated to be about twenty-three percent of the pottery production for the entire country. By 1920, a total of forty-eight potteries operated in the area employing nearly 7,000 hands with an astounding $30 million output. (Goldberg, 55) It was not an exaggeration when the *Trenton Times* once said that in the early 1920s, when the industry was still flourishing, as many as 7,000 cheesesteaks were sold daily to Trenton's pottery workers on their lunch hour. However, the industry began going downhill as early as 1927 (Goldberg 13).

For about eighty years, the Trenton pottery industry contributed a lot to the prosperity of the region and to the nation. Three major advances the industry achieved had made that growth possible. They were the successful commercialization of white ware, the introduction of sanitary ware and the development of Belleek. (Goldberg, 55) It was the success of the white ware and sanitary ware that set the stage for the making of American Belleek.

William Young, an English immigrant, was credited as one of the potters who introduced white ware into Trenton. His products shown at the 1854 Exhibition of American Manufacturers in Philadelphia attracted a lot of attention. Soon, many potters followed suit in producing this inexpensive utilitarian ware. By 1870, thirteen out of the fifteen Trenton potteries were emphasizing white ware production (Goldberg 13).

Another English immigrant, Thomas Maddock, successfully marketed sanitary ware in 1874. He was largely responsible for devising the flushing mechanism used in today's toilets. His company later became American Standard Inc. By 1891 almost all of the sanitary ware sold in this country originated in Trenton (Potteries of Trenton Society, 7).

The commercial success of these two products had made Trenton a mature training ground for native potters and attracted many foreign potters with expertise to offer. It provided Trenton with immense wealth, not just in terms of capital, but also in terms of skill, creative talent, experience, and physical facility. By 1880 Trenton's pottery industry was ready to embark on a more ambitious agenda. All the ingredients needed for the making of highly admirable porcelain were in place. All it took was someone who had the courage to take the lead to bring pottery making to the next level. John Hart Brewer was that someone who first seriously engaged himself in achieving the dream of making a porcelain ware so fine that it would rival the foreign imports at the time. That dream must have taken a more concrete shape when he could appreciate the famous Irish Belleek in person. As he was showing his products at the 1876 Centennial Exposition in Philadelphia, Irish Belleek made its debut in America at the same show. To achieve his dream, he would have to do it at the expense of his commercial success. His company was enjoying great success in granite ware, cream ware and parian ware. His famous parian pieces, the Baseball Vase, the Pastoral Vase, and the Bust of Cleopatra, to name a few, were hailed as being the best ever made in this country. By shifting gears and putting these cash cows in the back seat, he was taking a huge personal risk. Belleek was both expensive to make and purchase. Even if he succeeded in making them, they would not be as profitable as the more utilitarian wares he was making. If he failed, his reputation would be at stake and his company might not be able to get back on its feet. Undaunted, he started experimenting with this new technique in 1882 with the help of William Bromley, Jr. When he was not satisfied with the partial success after one year, he enlisted the help of the more experienced Bromley Sr. (Barber, 215). There was no documented date as to when Ott & Brewer finally succeeded in making Belleek. We believe that their success might have happen in late 1883 or early 1884 because the next company, Willets Brothers, started making Belleek (also with the help of the elder Bromley) around late 1884 or early 1885. In time, Belleek-making spread to many other potteries in Trenton as well as in Ohio. Even though Ott & Brewer had, through the year, improved the body and glaze of its Belleek ware and was considered the industry's leader in terms of quality and artistic value, it was forced to close in 1892 due to labor unrest and nationwide economic depression. In 1929 the Irish Belleek Pottery Limited was successful in a suit filed against the Morgan Belleek China Company of Canton, Ohio, to stop it from using the name "Belleek". Since then the Irish firm had the exclusive right to the name "Belleek" and the American Belleek era was officially over.

The 1930s also saw the demise of Trenton's pottery industry as a whole. The first factor was a six-month long strike by potters in Trenton in 1894. This was followed by another potters' strike demanding a pay increase in 1895. Both had a long-lasting effect on production efficiency and costs. In addition, World War I greatly reduced the labor pool at home. The resistance to the introduction of new labor saving technologies by workers and the increasing use of plastics by consumers were another two factors that contributed to the failures of a lot of potteries. Finally, the successful law suit by the Irish company to prohibit American potters from using the name "Belleek," and the Great Depression in the 1930s also played important roles in the failure of the industry. By the end of World War II, only eighteen potteries were listed as being in operation.

Today, only one company from the American Belleek era has survived. It is Lenox.

Collecting American Belleek and Price Guide

Collecting American Belleek vs. Imported Porcelain

When we first saw an American Belleek vase in 1976 while we were doing an antiques show in Miami Beach, Florida, we thought it was a porcelain vase made somewhere in Europe because its quality was excellent. Not knowing that it was a CAC vase decorated by a professional artist, the mark on the bottom looked strange to us at the time. We knew that it was not an Asian porcelain vase because we were particularly familiar with them. Our entire booth was filled with Chinese and Japanese porcelain. The decoration on that vase was like an oil painting of roses, and we believed it was a characteristic only of European porcelain makers. The dealer who happened to be set up next to us was very friendly, and he took the time to give us a lecture on porcelains that were made in America, more precisely made in Trenton, New Jersey. By the end of the show, we had traded an old Chinese vase for it. That vase was our first American Belleek.

The show in Miami Beach was a tremendous one. There were hundreds of dealers selling fine porcelain. Most of those porcelains were from overseas, mainly from Europe. We wandered around for a few days asking other dealers about American Belleek, but no one seemed to pay much attention to them. As artists doing oil paintings, we thought the rose vase was wonderful. Even though we *felt* that trading one of our better Chinese vases for it might not be wise, we traded it in anyway. We then began to wonder why American collectors would rather buy something made in foreign countries while staying away from the fine porcelain made in their own backyard.

When we compared American Belleek with some fine foreign porcelain, such as the Chinese Sung or Ming porcelain or those made by KPM or Meissen, we could understand that they are different in style and decoration. However, when we looked at other imports, especially Limoges or Nippon, we were really confused. Both

Limoges and Nippon are plentiful, and their qualities are no better than American Belleek. While each of them has its own uniqueness, these three types of porcelain have a lot in common. Many of their shapes such as plates, mugs, tankards, tea sets, and cups & saucers are similar to each other. They also used similar subjects (flowers, portraits, birds, landscapes) and decoration techniques (gilded rims & handles, hand-painted decorations, and transferred-prints). Sometimes one cannot tell what they are without looking at their marks.

We have no intention of discouraging collectors from collecting Limoges, Nippon, or any other foreign porcelain since everyone has his or her interest in something. We only want to bring to the attention of collectors that there is something really good at home waiting for them to discover and collect as well. So, we asked ourselves why American collectors would prefer items made in foreign countries over porcelain made by their ancestors? Why are Limoges and Nippon commanding higher prices than American Belleek? Aren't foreign companies still producing porcelains that are available through American companies anytime and at any quantity while there are very few pieces made in America? According to the rules of collecting antiques, isn't it true that rarer pieces command higher prices if they are comparable in quality, rather than the other way around? Isn't Americana becoming hot? Finally, since relatively few art porcelains are being made in America, wouldn't this be the time to collect American Belleek?

Let's point out a few more good things about American Belleek. For those collectors who enjoy art made by Europeans, many American Belleek pieces have the same high quality because many potters came from Europe, bringing with them the techniques that they learned in their native countries. There were also many Americans who went overseas to learn the skills before returning home. More importantly, there were many talented artists in America who developed their skills at home. The result was that we got the best of all.

Furthermore, if you look at the pieces made by Ott & Brewer, you will find that many of their designs are not only unique, but also outstanding and very artistic. Their gilt-painted pieces with artistic shapes are especially appealing (Plate 205); their decorations, like the butterflies on tea sets and cups and saucers, are truly lovely (Plates 240 and 223); their designs of unusually shaped pitchers are exceptionally creative (Plate 244); their eggshell pieces are as good in all aspects as those pieces made by their major foreign competitors (Plate 219); their quality and detail are all top notch; and the list goes on.

If you are still not convinced, then compare similar items made overseas with the CAC-Lenox porcelains such as the portrait vase (Plate 7), the Morley plates (Plates 27 to 39), the pink chrysanthemums vase (Plate 153), or the pieces made by Willets such as the rose vase by Marsh (Plate 257), the hibiscus jar (Plate 254), and the cup and saucer (Plate 281). On the other hand, if you are looking for less expensive pieces, there are many pieces that were decorated by amateurs readily available. They are just as good as many Limoges and Nippon items. What more can you ask for?

Competition

From the mid-1870s to the early 1930s, companies making American Belleek faced competitors not only from abroad but also amongst themselves. Competition was incredibly fierce in their product shapes and designs. Although many people suggested that American potters mainly imitated the shapes and patterns from their Irish counterparts, in fact many shapes and designs made by both European and American companies were imitations of silver and metal wares made around the globe (Vickers) from as early as the Roman, Egyptian, and Greek empires, and the Han Dynasty of China. All of these companies made similar products such as tankards, ewers, urns, and vases. These products were sometimes so identical that it was impossible to tell who made them without looking at their marks. For instance, very often today it is difficult to differentiate if a tankard was a Limoges or American Belleek unless a collector looks at the maker's marks. Although there were subtle differences between some sets of eggshell cups and saucers made by Ott & Brewer and Willets, their overall appearances are as similar as twins: only their parents and close friends are able to tell them apart. Even amongst smaller companies, such as Coxon and Morgan, competition was as bad as those amongst the larger ones. They produced not only the exact same shapes and sizes of products, but also used the exact same designs and patterns. Plate 313 illustrates an example. Two different companies made this cup and saucer set; the cup was made by Morgan while the saucer was made by Coxon. Both pieces used the EXACT same transfer pattern. Such fierce competition hurt not only the companies but also the industry as a whole. The market was saturated, consumers were confused, prices and profits dropped, and everyone went out of business in a short time. Even in today's market of antiques, if there is an excessive supply of certain products, prices will be suppressed no matter how good the product is. We will discuss this subject under *Silver and Silver Overlay Items*.

Factory & Professionally Decorated Items vs. Amateur Decorated Items

Naturally, most collectors consider factory and professionally decorated items more valuable and more highly collectible than amateur decorated pieces. The main issue is how to distinguish a factory or professionally decorated item from an amateur decorated example. We have come across numerous occasions where a dealer attempted to sell us pieces by stating that they were professionally decorated, when in fact they were not.

Although we define a professional artist as someone who makes a living by painting and selling artwork daily, we must also recognize that some amateurs are more talented and creative than professional artists. Several part time artists (also called amateurs) who exhibit their work at our gallery are of top quality in every aspect, such as composition and design, color management and application, object proportion, techniques, details, and overall presentation. Therefore, oftentimes we consider the collectible value of such items that are "beautiful and well decorated" to be higher than those that are "poorly decorated," regardless of whether those items were decorated in a factory, in studio, by professional artists or so called amateurs.

The quality of factory decorated items is usually superior to those produced by studios, especially ones that come in sets. Factories generally maintained higher standards and quality control over production. On the other hand, CAC/Lenox, Ott & Brewer, and Willets did not employ a large number of artists to decorate their items. In fact many of their products were sold as white or undecorated wares to other studios and amateurs. For this reason, there are significantly more non-factory items available on the market than factory decorated ones. Given that there are only twenty-four hours in a day, no matter how diligently an artist worked, one could only decorate a limited number of items a day. Let's consider one of the most renowned artists of that era, William Morley, who joined Lenox in 1900 and worked with the company until 1934.

Around 1902, Lenox began to take on the European service item market by offering service plates decorated by its top artists. These plates were so well received that Lenox increasingly turned its attention to complete sets of dinnerware and, in 1906, changed its name from Ceramic Art Company to Lenox Incorporated to reflect the new direction (Lenox, Inc.). Among those decorated plates, William Morley's work was considered the best, and thus, today we call the plates he decorated the *Morley plates* in his honor. In our opinion, Morley plates are excellent items to collect. Not only were they artistically and skillfully decorated, but they also represent an important part of American Belleek history, for their success helped influence Lenox to change its name. A collector who wants to collect Morley plates will find more game and fish plates than floral plates. We happen to personally value the floral plates more than the game and fish plates mainly because of the rarity of them, although some collectors may feel differently depending on their personal preference and opinion.

Although *good and beautifully* decorated American Belleek done by professional studios should command prices close to factory decorated examples, it is sometimes too difficult to determine if an item is beautifully decorated or not as it becomes a matter of subjective versus objective. For example, the urn which was decorated with women and cupids (Plate 164) is as good as other urns that were decorated by factory artists. Most factory-decorated items, such as service items (pitchers, tea sets, cups and saucers) as well as small items (salt and pepper shakers and fountain pens), were not signed by artists. There are some exceptions, such as Morley plates or some plates signed by F. Fenzel. It is more likely that decorative items such as vases and urns have a greater chance of being signed by a factory artist, although we have seen more unsigned pieces than signed ones. On the other hand, most, if not all, amateurs signed their works. For this reason, if we find two items, one has beautiful decoration and was unsigned while the other one has poor decoration and was signed, we personally favor the unsigned item. Of course, those pieces signed by factory artists such as W. Marsh, H. J. Nosek, and W. Morley are definitely the most desirable pieces to collect. Whenever possible, we do not let them slip away.

One of the benefits of collecting high quality or factory pieces is that they are not easily reproduced. Even if the importers were to reproduce items of such high quality, the profit margin for reproducing them is expected to be lower than reproducing pieces of lesser quality. Furthermore, if a company wants to reproduce such high quality items, it would be more beneficial for the company to market them under its own brand. Another benefit of collecting the factory pieces is that they have better investment potential than those with poor quality or made by amateurs.

Methods of Decoration

Before we discuss the methods of decoration in detail, we want to point out one simple element of decorating porcelain that might have been overlooked by other authors: the different kinds of clay used to make porcelain may somehow affect the end results of the decorations because the colors of the porcelain bodies may vary slightly. It is just like the color of pure porcelain is different from that of bone china. Therefore, if an artist used certain color pigments on porcelain made with clays in Trenton, New Jersey, after firing, the colors may turn out to be slightly different from the same color pigments that he or she used on porcelain made with clays in Zanesville, Ohio. We learned this information from an art pottery studio in China several years ago, when an artist demonstrated to us the colors of two different vases made with clays from two places a few hundred miles apart. Therefore, an experienced collector may be able to differentiate a real American Belleek made in Trenton, New Jersey, from a new reproduction made overseas. The key is to handle pieces of porcelain made in as many different places as possible.

There are two main categories of porcelain decoration: one is hand painting and the other is transfer-printing. Of course, there can also be a combination of both. Naturally, hand-painted items command higher prices if both have the same quality of artwork. We would prefer a transfer-printed item over a *poorly* decorated item done by an amateur. Buying a transfer-print item has an advantage: it was almost always decorated in the factory and its quality is more consistent. The more desirable items than total transfer-print items are those with a combination of transfer-print and hand decoration, such as the Virginian items made by Lenox.

Hand painting can be in colors or in gold. It can also be a hybrid of both, such as those decorated by a combination of hand painting and transfer-print. Color painting is easy to tell simply by looking at the item. Some color decorations can have the effects of looking like enamel if they were applied with raised beads that have the luster glaze on them. Lenox used this method of enamel decoration quite often on their service wares. They are very labor intensive and the overall result is very pleasant.

There are three types of gild decorations. The first one is by *flat brush*. This is like color painting except the artist uses gold instead of color paints. The second method is *raised gold*, also called *gold paste* or *gilt*, painting. This method requires rigorous training and was usually done in the factory. They are very difficult to produce and most amateurs could not achieve the desired level of quality unless they were well-trained artists. If you look at the pieces carefully, they are indeed very beautiful. More importantly, they blend in well with almost every item that has some gilded decorations. Ott & Brewer used this technique more often than the other two companies. The most desirable pieces are those that used raised gold as outlines for a color design, and the design was then filled in with color. Both Ott & Brewer and CAC/Lenox produced excellent examples of this method. (Plates 114, 153, 207, 250). The last method is *etched gold*. The technique is to first lay out the design, then apply a coating of protective substance on the areas where they are not to be etched. The item is then bathed in acid until the unprotected areas are etched to a desired level. Finally, the gold is applied to the etched areas, and the item is fired. This technique required professional expertise that not every studio could handle. CAC/Lenox used the method very often on their service wares. This method was mainly used to decorate the borders of the service wares such as dinner plates. Decorative wares with etched gold, such as vases, are very rare (Plate 157).

Transfer-print was used more often by foreign potters such as R. S. Prussia and Nippon, especially with portrait decoration. Much of American Belleek was hand decorated. In fact, when CAC/Lenox decided to expand its business into the service ware market in 1902, most of their items were still hand decorated. The plates, especially the Morley plates, were so successful that CAC/Lenox turned its attention to selling more service wares and in 1906 changed its name to Lenox to truly reflect its business. In 1910, it introduced a few patterns with transfer-print and hand enhanced decoration to the market. (Lenox

Inc. website 2002) Among the early patterns introduced by Lenox in the early 1900s were *Virginian* (1910), *Mt. Vernon* (1911), *Tuxedo* (1912), *Stanford* (1916), *Lowell, Mandarin,* and *Ming* (1917), *Autumn* (1919), *Colonial, Fair Mount, and Orchid* (1920). Among the above-mentioned patterns, Virginian was probably the most expensive pattern while Mount Vernon (also nicknamed "*Poor Man's Virginian*") was second. Mandarin, which had some hand-applied decorations, was much better than another pattern, Ming. Ming was entirely decorated with transfer-print. However, the Ming pattern lasted for fifty years, which we believe was due to its lower prices, which allowed it to survive the Great Depression and WWII. Another pattern produced by Lenox entirely with transfer-print that lasted almost as long as Ming was Lenox Rose (1934). There are thousands of both Ming and Lenox Rose pieces available in the market at any given time. Therefore, to collect items with such huge availability, one has to be more selective. For example, we only collect Lenox Rose pieces with a *pink* wreath mark, as we believe that they were the first pieces made in this pattern.

Many factory items, especially transfer-print pieces, were produced in mass quantity while hand decorated ones were produced in limited quantity. Hand decorated items are in fact one of a kind even if an artist such as William Morley painted many similar items. For instance, we have two Morley Rose cup and saucer sets (Plate 23). If a collector puts these two sets together and compares them, he or she will find that there are differences in the sizes of roses and the shapes of leaves. This is also true for the Morley plates and most items made by Ott & Brewer. We show several similar sugar bowls (Plates 234 to 239) by Ott & Brewer with different decorations of flowers and butterflies in this book. Also, if a collector compares the Morley plates, he or she will find that each plate is in fact different from the others. (Plates 27 to 32, and 107 to 112). On the other hand, even though items such as the CAC/Lenox Virginian or Mount Vernon pattern were enhanced by hand after the transfer-print was applied, they can only be considered as factory decorated items rather than artist decorated items. These items also look different from one another. However, there is a slight difference between hand-decorated pieces and hand-enhanced pieces. The former were decorated by good artists with high artistic skills to make the piece a work of art, at higher production costs. The latter pieces were also hand-decorated (after the initial transfer-print decoration), but by factory staff or designers and most likely by a group of lesser-known artists in the form of an assembly line to reduce costs. We would like to classify these two groups of items as artist decorated items and factory-decorated items. We have no intention of downgrading the factory-decorated items but we must also acknowledge the fact that they are different in many aspects. Artists' signatures on the items, except those decorated by amateurs, do affect the values of the pieces. However, one should keep in mind that many factory artists did not sign the items, especially those made by Ott & Brewer. In fact, we have only seen one signed Ott & Brewer item since we first started collecting American Belleek in 1976. It is our belief that, in the long run, good artist decorated items should command higher prices than factory decorated ones.

Decorations can be applied underglaze or overglaze. While some American Belleek items were decorated on bisque without glaze, most of them were decorated with glaze. Glaze can be satin or glossy. If a glazed item was decorated before it was glazed and fired, it has a greater chance of failing to achieve the desired colors. In other words, there is a greater rate of defect. For this reason, most American Belleek was decorated after the porcelain body was glazed and fired, or so called overglaze. After the decoration on the glazed body was finished, the porcelain was fired again under a lower temperature to make the decoration permanent. If the porcelain was not fired after decoration, it is called cold-painted, and the paint falls off easily. While there is no difference in price between underglaze and overglaze, many collectors prefer satin over glossy glaze. Ott & Brewer produced more satin pieces than both CAC/Lenox and Willets. Those items are always in very high demand.

Many American Belleek pieces were produced from molds, especially those made by Lenox after 1930s. Although these pieces have their own beauty and merits, we prefer to call them design items rather than decorated items. The much more delicate items were those with applied handwork on the porcelain bodies. These items were very difficult and time consuming to make. Often, the rate of defect was so high that their initial selling prices were much higher than those fully decorated pieces without hand-applied decoration on them. Fewer pieces were available in the market as well. As a result, they also command higher prices today. Hand-applied decorated items damage easily after leaving the factory, and it is rare to find a piece without some form of damage and/or restoration. Many serious collectors do not limit themselves only to mint condition pieces, or they will not be able to collect a wide variety of art porcelain made in America. If they only look for mint pieces, their collection may be limited to *common pieces*, especially if they collect those made by Ott & Brewer. We also discuss this topic under "Condition and Restoration."

Subjects and Styles of Decoration

In collecting art ceramics, porcelain, and pottery, the subject of decoration is one of the factors in determining the value of each individual item. In most art pottery such as Rookwood and Roseville, items decorated with animals, landscapes, or portraits are valued more than those with birds, insects, geometric designs, or flowers, assuming all other factors such as condition, size, and age are the same. In collecting American Belleek and, to some extent, imported porcelain like Limoges and Nippon, more collectors prefer items decorated with flowers and portraits providing that the portraits are done of females and not monks. Roses seem to be the most popular flowers while others such as orchids, lilies, and violets are also in demand. Pieces that were decorated with beautiful female figures or portraits and enhanced with flowers are the most desirable items. The key is to collect items that are *"beautiful."*

Collectors' preferences and tastes change from one period to another due to many factors, including economic, social, and/or trends. However, we believe that *beautiful* pieces will always be the best collectibles in any given time. Their value will always be substantiated and thus they are the best investment in the world of antiques. In the late 1800s to early 1900s, items with monks were popular. In the long run, these items are the least desirable in many aspects. Imagine that a collector has a hundred floral pieces displayed in his or her home. He or she then adds a few items with monks among the flowers. The entire display is no longer in harmony. It is true that a collector may want to start a collection of monks. But then how appealing would it be to have a house full of monks in every self and cabinet? Also, the number of collectors that would actually seek such pieces in the long run would be considerably less, thus affecting the appreciating value according to the actual demand.

In American Belleek, items with decorations of Native Americans are seldom seen in the market. However, like those decorated with monks, they are not highly desirable, although items with Native Americans may command high prices in other category such as art pottery. Animal and scenic design pieces are also quite rare, especially ones made by Ott & Brewer. Items with birds and to some extent insects (butterflies and dragonflies) are more common, but they are excellent items to collect as they fit well with flowers. Again, keep in mind that many American Belleek items were decorated by amateurs, and rarity is only one of the factors that determine the value and collectible nature of an item; beauty is the key.

Finally, the style of decoration also affects the value of American Belleek items. In collecting art pottery, arts and crafts style may be preferred over art nouveau and Victorian ones. On the contrary, American Belleek items that are decorated in art nouveau and Victorian styles, especially those items that are painted in classical techniques, are valued higher than those decorated in arts and crafts style.

Decorated Items and White Wares

Over the years, we have had numerous discussions with many collectors and dealers about one of the reasons that led to the dismal popularity of American Belleek in the antiques and collectibles market. It was the poor quality of many amateur decorated items that misled people to associate American Belleek with inferior porcelain. Some decorations were so poor that Robinson & Feeny said in their book, "it might be a kindness to break them." (Robinson, 24). Well, this solution may be too extreme, but unless you are collecting a "piece of history," you may want to consider letting them go to other homes. On the other hand, American Belleek is indeed so beautiful that even many modern Chinese porcelain designers admire it. Throughout this book, you will find that most pieces illustrated here are of top quality. There are only a few pieces that were not professionally decorated. We included them in this book because of their unusual shapes, such as the orange bowls (Plate 289). In fact, like many collectors of American Belleek whom we spoke to, we prefer non-decorated pieces (or so-called white wares) over poorly decorated pieces. The history and beauty of white wares can be traced back to 1925.

At the Exposition Internationale des Arts Decoratifs et Industriels Modernes held in Paris in 1925, the Swedes concentrated on tableware, mainly white porcelain, notable for its attention to simple forms and texture rather than decoration. (Atterbury 1982, 220). In 1934, the Museum of Modern Art in New York held an exhibition of "Machine Art" that included a large section on Household Accessories, where Lenox exhibited some commercial white porcelain plates and an absolutely cylindrical porcelain vase. The Director of the Museum invokes Plato's dictum that geometrical shapes had absolute rather than relative beauty. (Atterbury 1982, 222). Many undecorated porcelains, especially those made during the period from the 1930s to the 1940s by Lenox, have their own special uniqueness. The designs on those pieces express their beauty without the distraction of colors. During that period, which, in fact, continued throughout the 1950s, Americans preferred and enjoyed these white porcelains with muted and elusive patterns for their dual advantages of showing off the quality of porcelain and not dating a piece. (Atterbury 1982, 224). In other words, their beauty is not confined to a certain period or influenced by commercial trends. Like bread and butter fitting well in every meal, they fit well with every setting. We show a few samples of them in this book.

Quality Controls

From our experiences, opinions that we've received from dealers and collectors, and readings of some authors such as Robinson & Feeny, we concluded that among the three companies, namely CAC/Lenox, Ott & Brewer, and Willets, Lenox had the best quality control on their products while Willets had the worst. The quality of CAC/Lenox's factory decorated products, especially their service wares such as dinner and lunch wares (except the Ming line), were very consistently maintained with high standards. Ott & Brewer also did an excellent job on quality control, especially on their decorated eggshell items and art wares. We never encountered a non-factory decorated Ott & Brewer item, although some authors say that the company did have a few pieces that were not decorated in the factory. We understand that Ott & Brewer's items command the highest values because of their high quality, their short business life, and their limited availability, as well as being the first company to make American Belleek. However, we cannot understand why Willets items are being sold at higher prices than those of CAC/Lenox. It is a myth to us that it will not last forever because serious collectors will eventually realize that they have no reason to pay a premium price for a Willets item if a CAC/Lenox item is as good as, if not better than, a Willets piece. In fact, some artists, such as George Houghton, Walter Marsh, and Hans John Nosek, worked for both companies. In our opinion, both CAC/Lenox and Willets items should be valued about the same with "all things (condition, size, decoration, etc.) being similar." We prefer not to say "all things being equal" because the items were made by two different companies, after all. One last note: we have noticed that there are considerably more Willets items decorated by amateurs available in the market than CAC/Lenox items. There are more unmark Willets items sold in the market than those of the other two companies, which is another indicator that Willets did not maintain tight control on the quality of their products. Lenox also had unmarked items, but they were left unmarked on purpose. If the items were left purposefully unmarked, it was either because they were too small to mark (like the fountain pens) or for other obvious reasons (like the door knobs and knife handles).

Unmark Items and Their Desirability

Unmarked items by CAC/Lenox and Ott & Brewer are rare, especially for those pieces that were made with the intention of bearing no markings, such as fountain pens, mirrors, and shakers. On the other hand, many items made by Willets were not marked. We could only identify them by their shapes and the colors of the porcelain made during those years. Over the years, we have been asked so many times by collectors if an unmarked item is worth collecting, and our answer is yes. As collectors ourselves, we collect the items or antiques not solely for resale. We enjoy them. If we can identify an item as an American Belleek, say Willets, we never hesitate to buy it. Keep in mind that in the world of antiques, not every fine antique was marked. Many unmarked antiques, collectibles, or ceramics are worth much more than marked ones. For instance, an unmarked Grueby (1907-1911) pottery vase can go for tens of thousands of dollars, while a marked Owens (1896-1907) vase could be worth less than one hundred dollars. It all depends on the items rather than on the marks.

Condition and Restoration

When collecting American Belleek and other kinds of antiques, condition is among the most important factors in determining the value of an item. However, it should not be the only factor used to value an item. Even an expensive old painting worth millions of dollars may not be mint. When we consider using the word mint, it is quite subjective. Some major auction houses describe the condition of an item "mint, perfect, and pristine" as "the item is in the same condition that it was at time of manufacture," regardless of if the items had factory defect(s) or even if the defect(s) are visible. On the other hand, we were once told by a customer that when an item leaves the factory, it is not mint anymore. This might be too extreme of a condition to impose on an antique. We were also told by another collector that *crazing* were in fact cracks, and a crack was a crack regardless what name you put on it. We do not want to get into this type of argument. So we define an item in mint condition as if the item is free of cracks/hairlines (except normal crazing), chips (large or small), repairs, and without major factory defects.

Some collectors collect only mint pieces, which in fact limits the depth and scope of their collections. However, if an item is a common piece, then collecting a mint one makes sense, and a collector should by all means do so. A common piece is usually less expensive and appears often. If a collector does not buy it when the item surfaces in the market, he or she can always find another one soon. If a collector of means scoops up 100 common pieces of American Belleek in haste rather than taking time to collect less common, factory decorated items, that would not be a collection to be particularly proud of, especially if those pieces are full of amateur decorations. Also, a common item is not as good an investment as a scarce one. On the other hand, a rare piece may appear only once in a blue moon. If a collector lets it slip by, he or she might never find another one again. So a rare piece with small defects deserves serious consideration by collectors.

When a rare item, such as an Ott & Brewer pitcher with nice hand applied decorations, has some defects, our considerations are always as follows: what kinds of defects are they (chip or crack), how large are they, where are they, and can they be restored? If the defects are restorable, chances are we will acquire it if the price is reasonable. Now, how do we decide if a price is reasonable or not? We will deduct a value of fifteen to twenty percent plus restoration fees for a rare piece. In other words, let's assume a pitcher without defect is worth of $2,000. If it has minor defects and the restoration fee is $250 in order to have it properly done, we would consider a price of $1,350-$1,450 to be reasonable. If it has already been restored nicely, we would pay $1,600-1,700 for it. If the piece is a common item, such as a Willets 5" mug with

decorations of grapes, we most likely would pass on it. We wouldn't want to spend any money on restoring a common piece because the restoration fees could be more than the value of the item itself (or even the mint condition value).

Furthermore, small factory defects, light scratches, and wear to the gilded area must also be considered when buying a common item. However, we will consider these factors lightly on rare items, unless such minor defects appear in an obvious area that seriously detracts from its beauty. For example, some service wares such as a dinner plate would most likely have some knife marks and wear to its gilded rim. If it is, say a Lenox Rose plate, we will try to discount it more. If it is, say, a Morley plate, we may accept it without too much discount. Some collectors have suggested that gilded areas with wear should be regilded, either temporarily or permanently. We like the idea but believe that it should be up to the individual collector to decide. However, if the item is regilded permanently, such "restoration" should be disclosed to the buyer in the future. One might be able to tell if an item was regilded by trying to find out if the gilded area has some small scratches under the gold. Also, the colors of the new and old gold are usually slightly different. Some collectors (and authors) suggest that if the gold area on the piece looks new, it was most likely regilded. However, this is not always the case, as we have seen numerous times that many pieces were so well kept by collectors that they looked brand new and mint. In fact, many items shown in this book look as if they were brand new, and they have not been regilded.

In general, a service item such as a dinner plate or a teapot would have a greater chance of being damaged than that of a decorative item such as a vase or a charger. Thus, a collector should require a better condition for decorative items than service items, especially the Ott & Brewer hand applied items or trays with scalloped rims. The devaluation on a vase with a nick would be far greater than that of an Ott & Brewer tray with a small chip. For instance, we would discount fifty percent on the vase but might only discount ten percent on the tray if the small chip is not on a very obvious place.

Finally, restored items may also be needed to complete a certain set. For example, if a tea set is composed of a teapot, a sugar bowl, and a creamer, and the creamer is missing, then buying a creamer with restoration may be a good move. The value of a complete set is usually higher than the sum of all pieces that are priced separately.

Rare, Novelty, and Commemorative Items

Although rarity is only one of the major factors in determining the value and desirability of an antique such as American Belleek, depending solely on rarity to decide if one should collect an item may not be in the best interest of any collector, even though it is still better to buy a rare item than a common one. As we suggested in "Condition and Restoration," a large collection of common pieces, especially amateur decorated common pieces, is far less substantial than a small collection of uncommon and rare pieces. In the end, most collectors find owning a small assortment of rarities to be a far greater source of pride than a large collection of everyday items.

One way of collecting rare items is to collect novelties such as fountain pens and door knobs. Another way is to collect commemorative items. However, there is a small difference in collecting these two types of American Belleek. Most novelty items were factory decorated and they are always a pleasure to own. Commemorative items, on the other hand, were both factory and nonfactory decorated. While almost all of the novelty items are universal, by which we mean they were not specifically designed for a special group or club, commemorative items were always made for a special occasion or society. Thus, novelty items are for everyone and commemorative items are not. For example, a fountain pen decorated with roses could be a great collectible for everyone. A cup and saucer set that was made to celebrate a special event for a particular institute, say a 50th reunion of a state university, may not be for everyone because such a set may not be of particular interest to collectors who are not the university's alumni. On the other hand, if the set was made for a special occasion, such as the celebration of Shakespeare's 100th birthday, then that set is more collectible because even an European collector might be interested in buying it. In other words, collecting commemorative items with universal appeal, such as the cup and saucer set made by Ott & Brewer for the New Orleans Exposition in 1885, or even the set made to commemorate the banquet of the Crockery Board of Trade of New York in 1897 (Plate 102) is more enjoyable. Also, some commemorative items were artistically designed while others were not. So if a commemorative item was beautifully decorated (Plate 100), one may consider collecting it as simply a *pretty* American Belleek instead of a commemorative item.

Silver and Silver Overlay Items

The history of the liner with a silver holder goes as far back as the early Han Dynasty of China (BC 204) or even earlier, although during that time entire vessels of this sort were made of metals in different sizes and shapes. Lenox, and to a lesser extent Willets, started to produce porcelain liners and sold them to silver companies such as Gorham and Mauser almost immediately after CAC began its business in 1889. Each porcelain liner came with a silver holder and (usually but not always) a silver saucer (Robinson). The silver parts were made separately by different silver companies to form a complete set. This product category was so successful that, over the next forty to fifty years, huge quantities of liners in different sizes and shapes were produced (Plate 60). They were sold mainly as wedding presents in sets of six, eight, or twelve, with or without carrying cases. Thus, the majority of the liners were white wares, decorated with only a gold band on the liner's inside rim. For this reason, the most common shape was the bell-shaped liner, although there were also barrel-shaped, hexagonal, and octagonal liners. There were also liners with other colors, but those were so rare that they are almost impossible to find today (Plate 59).

Some liners have decorations on them, such as the transfer-printed Tuxedo and Mandarin patterns. However, the most desirable liners are those with hand-decorated flowers, including the sets that were made by the Mauser silver company (Plate 49). The liners made to sell with Mauser silver were decorated with a garland of flowers inside the cups with an apple green color on the outside. Mauser sets never came with saucers. Decorated liners with or without silver holders are highly sought by collectors today, and prices could go as high as a few hundred dollars each. The highest price that we have noticed was a Mauser set that was sold on the internet for over $400 in October 2002. Most liners are small, from 1-1/2" to 2-1/4" in height and around 2" to 21/4" in diameter. There is a larger size for liners, and many collectors call them chocolate liners or cups. Their size is 3" x 3" (Plates 52 and 54). According to Robinson and Feeny, *"Chocolate cups are exceedingly rare."* They also mention that there are rumors of full size coffee cups or teacups, without giving the sizes; however, they might possibly be nonexistent. We have never seen one and cannot confirm their existence, either. Besides cup liners, Lenox also made other forms of porcelain liners and sold them to silver companies: butter dishes, honey pots, ramekin, soup cups, eggcups, bowls, etc. The production of liners ended around the mid-1940s. Some liners came with other metal (silver-plated, brass or copper) holders and saucers. These sets are not considered as desirable as the silver ones.

The liners with sterling holders and saucers are priced far below their reproduction costs today, and theoretically they are real bargains. However, there is a huge supply of liners (especially the wedding band design) available on the market today, and their prices have been severely suppressed. They were sold for around $25 to $35 each in the 1980s, and they are still being sold for around the same prices today, depending on the amount of silver and the names of the silver company. Only those liners with decorations other than the wedding band enjoy substantial appreciation of value, and we believe that it will continue to be this way for the coming years.

Many liners have monograms on either the silver holders or the saucers. Those sets with monograms are usually valued less than those without, but there are exceptions. If the monograms are single letters (say A or Z), there should be a minimum difference in values. If the monograms are words with special meanings, such as "WIFE" or "LOVE," they may in fact increase the set's value. In these cases, they can be given as gifts to someone for special occasions.

Aside from making liners for silver companies, Lenox also supplied them with blank porcelain items to decorate with silver overlay. These items included plates, teapots, sugar bowls, creamers, jars, pitchers, vases, and many other forms. The porcelain could be with or without decorations and in many colors, although the majority of them were white. Marked silver overlay items are naturally more desirable than those without the silver marks, and colored porcelains are worth a lot more than white wares. Yellow is the rarest color, followed by light blue, pink, light and dark green, red, orange (close to red but not exactly red), brown, peach (not pink), cobalt, ivory (not white), and white. There may be some other colors, but we have not encountered them so far. Silver overlay items have much greater potential than liners with silver holders and saucers, especially if there is a large amount of silver on the items or if they are decorated. The supply of silver overlay items is also not as plentiful as liners. Finally, Robinson and Feeny mentioned that *"Copper and gold overlay are also seen in rare instances…no prices for copper or gold overlay have been included here because none have been seen recently enough. In general, copper overlay items are worth about the same as comparable items with silver on them, and the gold would be worth more."* We have not seen any of copper or gold overlay items in the last ten years.

Collecting Items Made In U.S.A.

When we first began collecting and selling American Belleek in 1976, we were told by many friends (dealers and customers) that we should avoid buying any item with the mark, *"Made in U.S.A.,"* especially those with a gold mark, because they were *new*. The gold marks were used during the mid-1950s, and the items were only about twenty to twenty-five years *young*. Even items that have the green wreath mark with the words "Made in U.S.A." (CAC/Lenox Mark 16) were no good. We should buy only those that were close to being fifty years *old* (CAC/Lenox Marks 10 to 15). Well, times change. Those *new* items are now *old*; many of them are close to or even over fifty years old, already. After all, half a century is a long time. We believe that if an item survives that many years, it is certainly worth something, especially those that were decorated by renowned artists, such as the vase decorated with roses by Han John Nosek (Plate 11) or another decorated rose vase by George Morley (Plate 16). We believe the main objective of buying antiques or collectibles should be for pleasure. There are many Lenox products with gold marks or marks with the words "Made in USA" that have great collecting potential and deserve serious consideration by collectors. We include a few such pieces in this book.

Reproduction

Reproduction of American Belleek porcelain is still not a major concern today, although we believe that reproductions will eventually appear in the market, similar to what happened to Limoges, Nippon, Meissen, and other popular antiques, especially after they become more expensive and desirable. When that happens, Ott & Brewer and Willets reproductions of white porcelain will most likely be the first to appear. First, these items command good prices and can be very profitable if the reproductions are made overseas. Second, the shapes can be easily copied, such as bowls, cups & saucers, mugs, plates, tankards, and vases. In fact, the importer may not even have to copy the shapes because no one really knows how many shapes were made by those companies. For instance, every month we find some new shape that we have never seen before in the market. Third, except for items that were decorated by the factories or good artists, they are relatively easy to produce. However, many of the Ott & Brewer and Willets items are very unique, and their characteristics are quite outstanding. Those items are not only more difficult to reproduce, but they are also more costly to produce, especially those with unique characteristics such as the gilt-painted and matte pieces. An importer or wholesale house specializing in reproductions is more interested in making profit than art. They will avoid producing high cost and hard to make items, especially those that require high initial investment for production molds and tooling. On the other hand, since Lenox is still in business, we doubt any importer would mass reproduce any CAC/Lenox items. As we said before, they are in the market to make money, not legal trouble.

That being said, we personally believe that a collector should not be deterred by the possibility of seeing reproductions in the market. Otherwise, other fine antiques would not be as popular as they are today. Although the "reproducers" would do everything they could to imitate pieces so as to lure collectors, their aim is to make money. So they would most likely avoid reproducing high quality and high cost items. Every true and fine antique has its uniqueness, which is hard to reproduce. A factory mark can be stamped on any new porcelain vase, but the colors of its glaze and "feeling" on an old vase cannot be easily imitated. So do not follow the marks blindly. The key is to be educated and be prepared.

Artists

There were many artists working with the three major companies, CAC/Lenox, Ott & Brewer, and Willets, and we would like to briefly discuss a few of them. Most of the dating for the artists referred to Robinson and Feeny.

Lucien Boullemier was one of Lenox's best artists. He was famous for painting Victorian women with beautiful decorative backgrounds. He worked for Lenox from 1900 to 1906.

Dominic Campana worked for Pickard before he joined Lenox for about one year. He painted flowers as well as portraits. His works are very desirable.

Eugene DeLan worked for Lenox from the 1890s to 1915 and also had a studio with his partner, McGill, at one point. He painted mainly flowers.

F. Fenzel worked for Lenox from 1937 to 1946. His paintings consisted mainly of flowers and fruits. All of his works have the Lenox green wreath mark with Made in USA.

George Houghton worked for Willets before joining Lenox, and he worked there until the 1930s. He was known for his paintings of flowers but was also skilled at portraits and animals.

Sturgis Laurence worked for Lenox from 1893 to 1898 before he left the company to join Rookwood. He did mainly flowers but also worked on portraits.

Walter Marsh worked for all three companies and probably had his own studio at one point as well. He joined Lenox in 1903 and worked there for about six years, although Robinson and Feeny mentioned that he left Lenox in 1910. However, we have a few of his works with Willets dated at 1909 (Plates 257 and 259). He worked for Willets at least until 1913, as we have recently sold one of his works dated 1913. Before he joined Lenox, he worked for Ott & Brewer. He worked for Ott & Brewer sometime from 1883 to 1893, and we have one of his works (Plate 191) with Ott & Brewer. Marsh painted mainly flowers, and his works are highly sought by collectors. He almost always signed his works, except when he worked for Ott & Brewer. Ott and Brewer produced almost all of their items in the factory but did not encourage (or might not have allowed) artists to sign their works.

George Morley was William Morley's nephew. He went to Lenox with his uncle in 1900 and left the company around 1903. He returned to Lenox from 1930 to 1939. George painted mainly flowers and was not as famous as his uncle. However, many collectors prefer his works because they are much scarcer due to his short employment at Lenox. He did not always sign his works. We include several of his (signed and unsigned) works in this book.

William Morley was one of the best artists at Lenox. He first worked for Knowles, Taylor, and Knowles, and joined Lenox in 1900. He stayed at Lenox until his death in 1935. Although he was famous for his Morley plates, particularly the fish and game birds plates, his paintings of flowers were in fact more skillful and lively. Many collectors have begun to favor his floral works more than his fish and game birds works. He did not always sign his works.

W. T. Morris was an artist for Ott & Brewer before he founded his own company, Columbian Art Pottery, with F. R. Willmore in 1893.

Han John Nosek came to America in 1903. He first worked for Lenox from 1903 to 1908, left his job for other ventures, and returned to work for Lenox from 1939 to 1954. When he came to America, his name was Han Nosek, and therefore he signed his work with H. Nosek in his early employment. He changed his signature to J. Nosek in his later employment with Lenox after he was *Americanized* and used the American name, John. He was most famous for his portrait paintings, although he also did gorgeous paintings of flowers, especially roses. His works in the 1950s were as good as those done in the 1900s. H. J. Nosek also worked for Willets briefly. He, like other artists, did not always sign his works.

Sigmund Wirkner worked for Lenox from 1900 to the 1920s. His female portraits are highly sought by collectors and command very high prices.

Other artists working for Lenox include Baker, Broome, Clayton, Fauji, Bruno Geyer, Anton, and his son, Adolf Heidrich, Kuln, Martell, Sully, Swalk, and Witte. Willets artists also included Oliver Houghton, Renelt, and With.

Valuation of American Belleek

(A) Buying a Price Guide

There are many ways to buy an antique: at antiques shows and shops, flea markets, auctions, the internet, garage sales, estate sales, and through other channels. To make our discussion simple, let's consider buying antiques from one of these sources, auctions, because this is one of the most sophisticated places to buy. There are thousands of auctions held in the United States every week selling almost everything from livestock, houses, and equipment to antiques and collectibles. In the market of antiques and collectibles, many auctioneers do not give buyers sufficient time to preview the items before the auctions and to make decisions during the auctions. In addition, many auctioneers do not guarantee their items and sell their items in "as is" and "where is" condition. In other words, buyers will have to take their chance that an item they buy may have hidden defects, which the auction houses do not disclose nor give buyers sufficient time to inspect.

When bidding on a lot during an auction, there will be increments from the starting price to the hammered price. Some increments are small while others are big depending on how much the lot is. For example, if a certain lot is $500 plus fifteen percent buyer's premium, and the auction house's bidding increment is $50 until $1,000 is reached, then each bidding price will be $575, $632.50, $690…until it reaches $1,150. After that, each increment may become $100 plus buyer's premium depending on each auction house's policies. Many lots have reserves to *protect* consigners' investments. In other words, there will hardly be any bargains if the auction houses have reserves on their items.

Let's consider the following example in order to illustrate how it can be made more difficult for buyers to carefully make their decisions. If an auction house sells 100 lots an hour, each lot is allotted an average of thirty-six seconds for bidders to compete. Some lots last a few seconds if there is a lack of interest in those lots while other lots last a few minutes longer if there is considerable interest in them. Therefore, once a lot opens, a bidder has an average of a few precious seconds to decide if he or she wants to bid on it at all. If a decision has been made to join the bidding war, then at each increment, a bidder would have one or two seconds to decide whether or not to continue bidding. The price of a certain lot could jump from $575 to $1,150 in less than fifteen seconds. So buyers must know how much they are willing to pay for a certain lot, or they could get carried away easily. Therefore buyers need to be well prepared before they attend any auction. One way of getting prepared is to buy an antique guide.

There are many good antique guides available in the market. Many of the authors are not only experienced, but also thoughtful and professional. They specialize in their fields and have considerable knowledge concerning what they are writing about. Naturally, there are antiques guides that are not very useful for some collectors who collect only a few types of antiques. Those guides cover so many fields in one book that they lack the attention of details to every item and price in their guides. Also, if a guide contains tens of thousands of prices, but has only twenty to thirty items in each category, then a collector who buys such guides may not get much help from them. On the other hand, these guides are helpful tools for dealers who buy many types of antiques and need only a few price reference to update their prices or study the trends of certain categories. We buy these guides too. There are also some guides that simply collect auction results or look at one price offered by a dealer; and put those prices together in one book without carefully considering if the prices are a true representative sampling or simply *spot* prices. If an auction has, say, 600 lots in one day, then one could easily buy twenty auction catalogs from around the nation and produce a guide with 12,000 prices in a week, especially if it contains few pictures.

We define a *spot* price as "*a price of one individual item/lot that was sold at one auction or offered by a dealer at a particular moment.*" For example, if one item is sold at an auction at three o'clock in the afternoon on a certain date, such a price is called a *spot* price. It happened only at one auction and at one particular time. Another identical item may be sold at a different price at the same auction. In other words, an auction may have several similar or identical items, and each of which was sold at a different price. For example, at an auction, there are four Roseville Pinecone vases of the same shape, size, and identical condition. For whatever reason, each piece was sold at a different price. Each of these prices is a spot price. Furthermore, if three Willets vases (14" each) that have the same size, subject, and condition, and are in similar shape, but have three different qualities of decoration and are sold at three different prices (see discussion below), then again, each of these prices is a spot price. One last example is a particular item that is sold for a particular price. The price could be extremely low or high, such as an Ott & Brewer vase that was sold for $17,250 with an initial estimate of $1,450-$2,000 in 2002 at an auction house. If someone simply puts that price (and copies the descriptions from that auction house's catalog) in his or her book, that price is not an accurate representation, and should be considered a spot price. Therefore, if a buyer uses any of these prices as a guide to buy a similar or identical item, he or she may not have the best information to make an optimal decision.

Let's consider the following cases. In the summer of 1999, at a major art pottery auction in southwest Ohio, a 9" Roseville Carnelian II vase in a rich glaze of pink, purple, green, and tan was sold for $440 (ten percent buyer's premium included). A few days later, a similar vase at a smaller auction in central Ohio was sold for $275. At another major art pottery auction in the following month there were two more Carnelian II vases of the same size and shape, in identical condition, with similar colors, that sold for $357.50 & $385 respectively. Since then, we have seen a few more Carnelian II 9" vases in similar shape, colors, and condition from different auctions, shops, and antiques shows. The prices ranged from $242 to $467.50.

If we were to write an antique price guide of American art pottery, which price should we put on it, $242 or $467.50? If we simply put down *one* of these prices on the book, and said to our readers that "*this* is the price a collector should expect to pay for such a vase," would a collector agree with us without questioning its reliability? Let's pause for a moment and ask another question. Since we only described the vase as a "*9 inch Roseville Carnelian II vase in rich glaze of pink, purple, green, and tan*" without giving our readers a picture to refer to, do they have any idea what the vase would look like? Keep in mind that there are several different shapes of Carnelian II 9" vases and each one has a different value of its own depending on its shape. Generally, a bulbous vase is valued higher than a bud vase although both vases can have the exact same descriptions of size, colors, and conditions.

Here is another case. At the July auction in 1999, a 7" Weller Muskota flower frog with a woman and a swan was sold at $475. The following month, we went to the antiques show in Brimfield, Massachusetts. We found a similar Muskota flower frog and the price was $395. One of us was hesitant because there is a saying that "if it looks too good to be true, it probably is." We looked at it for more than ten minutes to search for any possible sign of repair. We could not find any. We trusted our experience and paid $355 (net of dealer's discount) for it. It turned out that we were right, for the item had no restoration of any kind. There was a huge price difference of more than $100 between them. Since then, we have seen another three similar Muskota flower frogs selling for $385, $495, and $550 (buyer's premium factored in) respectively. (Figure 1)

Now, if we were to write an antique price guide, again, which price should we put on it? The above examples were easy cases because each of these two items, the Roseville vases and the Weller flower frogs, is considered identical in its own merit. They both have the exact same shape, very similar colors, and identical condition. If we were to price these two items, we would either take an average price of all the prices we have gathered after eliminating the two extremes or use the middle prices as price ranges. Thus, we'll price the Roseville vase for $365 or $350-400; and the Weller flower frog for $450 or $400-500.

Now let's consider three Willets vases in the exact same size and condition. Also, each vase was decorated with the same subject, for example roses, except that one vase was decorated by an amateur and signed; the second vase was decorated by an unsigned professional artist; and the third one was decorated by a noted factory artist, say Marsh, and signed.

Assuming that the first one was sold at an auction for $715; the second one for $990; and the last one for $770, and we gave *one* of these vases as an example for our readers to use as a guide, they would get lost again. Keep in mind that we do **not** have any picture to show you the shape and quality of decoration. Instead, we simply copied the descriptions from the auction house's catalogs without telling you which year the auction was held, how

much buyer's premium (10%-20%) was charged, and how much shipping & handling costs might be required. We simply put them down as follows.
(1) Willets vase finely rendered with roses & leaves, 14", and artist signed. $715, or
(2) Willets vase finely rendered with roses & leaves, 14", and no artist signature. $990, or
(3) Willets vase finely rendered with roses & leaves, 14", and signed Marsh, $770.

You paid dearly for the guides because you wanted to buy a Willets vase. Do you have any idea what each vase looked like or how each vase was decorated? Now, how much are you going to pay for a 14" Willets vase with rose decoration?

Consider another scenario, which actually happened. We bought the first vase, which was decorated and signed by an amateur. We could not sell it after almost two years, and decided to get rid of it. We sold it for 467.50. We priced it for $550 and gave a fifteen percent discount to a dealer. At the same auction, we bought the unsigned vase for $990 with keen competition, and sold it for $1,150 in three months.

We also bought the Marsh vase at another auction for $770 in another state about three months after we bought the above mentioned two vases. It was an auction with no reserve on all of their items and they were not cataloged. There was no competition that night, and we bought it at a great price. We sold the vase to another dealer the next day for $1,000. When we went to an antiques show in Atlantic City, New Jersey, in the following week, we found that the dealer who bought the vase from us priced it for $1,995. She told us that she sold it for $1,600 to another dealer when we went back the next day to chat with her. Who knows how much the next dealer would price the vase for?

If someone looked at these auction prices and put any of them, say the Marsh vase, in his/her antiques guide as follows:
"Willets vase finely rendered with roses & leaves, 14", and signed Marsh, $770."
are you going to rely on it and wait for another Marsh vase of 14" for $770?

We drive more than 35,000 miles annually visiting antiques malls and shows. We also go to about thirty auctions a year. Many times we do not buy even a single item either because prices are too high or we could not find what we are looking for. If we do find an item(s), most of the time we pay a fair price for it. Sometimes we get carried away like other bidders, while at other times we get really good buys. Four years ago, we bought several pieces of majolica at one auction by paying twenty to thirty percent less than their market prices at that time. Two years later we bought a 15" Willets tankard and a 14" vase from the same auction house, which we sold recently for a huge loss because we did not see a short hairline or spider on them respectively at the auction. The

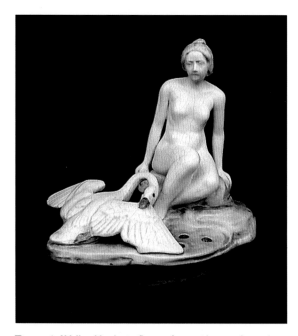

Figure 1. Weller Muskota flower frog with a nude and a goose, 7".

auction house's catalog said that they were mint and we did not carefully inspect the items. Although the auction house guaranteed all of their lots for thirty days, we did not find the defects until after their warranty expired. Last year, we paid almost forty percent more than a fair market price for a Rookwood iris vase that we later sold for a huge loss at a more reasonable price. As we mentioned above, during an auction, buyers are only given a few seconds to decide on the piece. In this case, its price jumped from $1,500 to $2,400 (+15%) in a few seconds. At the time, while our pedal was still up in the air, we were distracted by the bidder sitting next to us when she asked us a question. By the time we asked her to wait and put our pedal down; we were told that we *won* the auction. We were upset but understand that sometimes things happen for no logical reason, especially at auctions. Are we going to use these auction prices in our guide? Certainly not.

One more note about buying at auctions. We once read an author saying he was encouraged by his friend to bid on an item because his competitor was a dealer and he would not go wrong by beating the dealer. This could be true most of the time for collectors because dealers not only have to make a profit, but they also have much higher expenses to provide for traveling, operating (store or show rents), lost (broken or stolen) items, and other expenses. However, blindly following this rationale may get you in trouble too. Last year, one of our customers asked us to bid on her behalf for some of the items at an auction. She needed several items from that auction badly for personal reasons (we never ask our clients about their personal matters), and told us to get them at whatever prices for her from the auction. The result was that we bought the pieces at much higher prices than we normally would pay. If someone were to assume that, because we were dealers, then the prices we were willing to pay must be right and therefore they believe that they could pay even higher prices for those items that would lead them to have paid unreasonably high prices for those items if he or she won those auctions. Also, keep in mind that dealers make mistakes too. No one dealer knows all there is to know and they can easily get carried away from time to time when it comes to items that they may not be familiar with. Even if they are knowledgeable in a certain category, human mistakes happen as well, and sometimes things happen for no reason at all, such as with the Rookwood iris vase that we discussed before.

A collector can buy from many channels as we mentioned before. In general, auction prices are relatively lower, but they hold much higher risks even if for those that are experienced and know exactly how much they want to pay for an item. Internet prices also tend to be lower but from our personal experience, more than one third of the items are *not* as described, which indirectly pushes up the average prices for the correctly described

pieces. Shop & show prices tend to be higher unless you find an item that is priced incorrectly by a dealer who is not quite experienced in that area, and that still happens from time to time. On the other hand, buying from dealers has its advantages too. If you know a dealer who is honest and knowledgeable about a certain category, then buying from that dealer is probably a good move because you are paying a little extra money for their services. You most likely will pay a fair price for the item. You may also avoid getting an unnoticeably repaired piece or, in the worst case scenario, a reproduction. Keep in mind that in the long run, no one market or channel (auction, shops, internet, etc. ...) is superior to the other or the inferior ones would cease to exist. The key is to get yourself educated.

(B) How We Determined the Prices of the Items

Although the values in this book are only intended as a reference and not as a guide to set prices, we took every effort to gather as much information as we possibly could and carefully considered every aspect of each piece before we put a value on an item. Over the past two and a half year, we have surfed many websites; visited & attended antiques shows, auctions, small shops, large malls, and have spoken to many dealers and collectors. Taking the information we obtained through our travels and research, we combined it with the records of prices of the pieces that we have sold at our gallery. We then used both common sense and, whenever possible, statistical analysis to determine the values of the items and also eliminate those prices that fell too far away from the average ones. In addition, we used our personal experience, no matter how subjective it might be, and weighted factors such as rarity, subjects & quality of decoration, unique shapes, size, age, and artists to adjust them accordingly to reflect the current market values. The prices that we consider as spot prices at auctions and shops/shows are not used individually, especially those record high prices or unusually low ones. In other words, spot prices are used only as part of our data base to determine either average prices or price ranges. Also, prices that are considered unreasonably high or low are either eliminated or adjusted if we were able to find similar pieces as reference.

For example, a 10 inch gild-painted morning glories vase that was made by Ott & Brewer with an initial estimate of $1,450-$2,000 was sold at an auction for $17,250 in 2002. We would prefer not to put a value on it as we seriously doubt that it could be resold for that price in the future. Besides, it is not possible to put a fair market value on the vase, at least not until we see another three or four such vases sold in the open market in a reasonably short period, say six months to a year. A smaller Ott & Brewer vase (9") in similar glaze and subject, but with different colors and decoration, had an initial estimate of $1,150-$1,750, and was sold for $2,990 at the same auction. The hammered price of this vase is considered more reasonable, and we shall value that vase for $3,000-4,500. We value this vase at higher than the hammered price because several people that we talked to expressed their willingness to purchase a similar vase for such prices. We probably would do the same as well if we see another vase like it. Keep in mind that our willingness was somehow influenced by the record-breaking price. We would be willing to pay a higher price, hoping we would get a higher return in the future. In addition, we have seen two other similar (not exactly) vases priced for about $4,000 in the last six months at antique shows.

Another example was a Lenox open salt in the shape of a swan with a green wreath mark made around 1930, 2-1/2", with gilded rim, but *without* violets/purple on its body, sold over the internet for about $34 plus shipping while a similar one was sold on the same site for $83 plus shipping within a three month period. We also noticed that many similar pieces were sold for about $35-50 (plus shipping) each on the internet. They were priced from $40-$60 (buyer can expect a ten percent discount) at antiques shows or in shops in the last thirty months. Our estimate for such an item is $40-$50 (shipping and discount factored in) by eliminating the prices that fall on the two extremes. Since we have seen more than 200 pieces of this type of Lenox swans in the last two years, we have collected a large data set of prices for this item. Therefore, the price range for this item is relatively small because, statistically, a larger data set yields a smaller spread (difference) and results in a smaller range.

Before the internet played such an active role in selling and buying American Belleek, prices in the East Coast, especially in the mid-Atlantic and New England regions, tended to be higher than in other places. This is not the case anymore. In our valuation, we did not consider condition as a factor because all of the estimated values are based on good condition unless stated otherwise. We considered rarity, quality, decoration, and subject more important than size and age.

Although size and age are two very important factors in determining the value of an item, a larger or older item does not always command a higher value. A rare item, such as a fountain pen, is more valuable than a common-shaped mug. A 12" vase decorated by a renowned artist is worth more than an 18" vase decorated by an amateur. A 15" portrait vase decorated by H. J. Nosek with a green Lenox Made in U.S.A. mark dating from around the late 1940s is valued at a lot more than another 15" vase poorly decorated by an amateur with a CAC mark in 1889, and so on and so forth. We believe that this principle should also be used in our assessment of other antiques and collectibles. Let's consider buying an American art pottery such as a Roseville vase. A

Roseville Ferella vase (shape 507-9", circa 1931) or a Sunflower vase (shape 493-9", circa 1930) is valued much higher than a Donatello vase (shape 184-12", circa 1915) in the same mint condition.

For pieces that we have seen only once or twice, we tried to use cross referencing to determine their values, regardless of their hammered prices, which might be considered relatively high or low. For example, we valued an Ott & Brewer Gourd-shaped basket with scalloped rim & branch handle that was decorated with gilded dandelions (Plate 187) $1,750-2,500, regardless of how much the spot price was at an auction. We saw a similar basket sold for $1,800 (with several small chips on the rim) at an antiques show in the year 2000, and a couple of different shaped baskets made by the same company for $2,600 and $3,250 (both in great condition with only wear on the gilded handles) in 1999 and 2002 respectively. Note that the spread of its estimated value is larger than average because we do not have a large database to obtain a more precise range.

For rare pieces that we have no cross referencing on, we are usually hesitant to give a value. If we really have to put a price on such rarities, we can only value them based on our own opinion and those of the dealers & collectors we have talked to. In such cases, the price range is rather big. The Ott & Brewer vase that was sold for $17,250 in our discussion above is one example. Another example is a honey pot (Plate 321) made by Ott & Brewer. We have seen it only twice in the last decade and could not find similar pieces to compare its value. One was sold to a dealer for $1,100 (with hairlines) recently, while the second one was priced $2,250 (with no defect except minor wear of gold) by another dealer about six months ago. We would price it from $1,350-2,000 depending on its condition because this was what the dealers and collectors we spoke to were willing to pay should they see it somewhere in the future. Some prices in this book have a large range because we do not have sufficient data to effectively analyze them and to yield a more reasonable deviation, such as the Ott & Brewer honey pot we have just discussed. Therefore, for these types of unusual items, a collector must use his or her own judgment, including personal desires and reasons to value the pieces. Like buying stocks, a greater return on investment generally carries a greater risk. Other items such as the cups & saucers, we have sufficient data on them, and the price range (or so-called standard deviation) is relatively small.

For hand-painted and decorative items, collectors may not find the exact same pieces. Therefore, for similar but non-identical pieces such as vases, we used common sense to value them. For instance, a dealer sold a 17-1/2" CAC/Lenox vase that was decorated with violets by H. Nosek, for $2,850 in the year 2002. Another CAC/Lenox vase similar in size (18-3/4"), but with a slightly different shape and decorated with roses by W. Morley, went for

$2,415 at an auction in the year 2002. We sold a 19" vase that was also in a different shape and was decorated with orchids by Marsh for $2,200 in the year 2000. An unsigned rose decorated 18-1/2" vase that we suspect was decorated by a top artist (Figure 2) was sold for $2,500 by a dealer in the year 2002. Thus, we valued vases in similar quality and sizes for $2,350-2,850. For functional items, such as dinner plates and cups and saucers, similar methods were also applied to value them. For eggshell cup and saucer sets made by Ott & Brewer (Plates 225, 227, 229), we gave them the same estimated value even though their decorations were different. Also, a complete set is usually priced higher than the sum of each piece priced separately.

Many of the factors that we discussed in this section are explored in more detail in other sections of this book. So, when using this book as a guide, readers must carefully consider all factors, including personal ones, and exercise their own judgment before they decide if the price is right for them. Keep in mind that the correct value of an item for each individual collector is the one that he or she is willing to pay. We often paid a premium for an item that we either needed at that time or desired for personal reasons. For example, we bought a CAC urn (Plate 164) for about $650 at an auction (an unusually low price) two years ago and sold it for $1,000 within a week. We were so happy. Then, after a second thought, we regretted it for it is such a great piece of art. We recently bought this urn back because we want to show it in this book. We paid close to $2,800 for it. Our value for this piece is $2,250-$2,750, although we had an offer by a collector for $3,500 a few days after we bought it back. Another urn in the same size, shape, and condition, but decorated with white roses on only one side of the urn by a non-factory artist, was sold over the internet for $1,137 (plus shipping) in July 2002. Thus, the actual value of an antique or collectible depends on how much you need it and/or enjoy it.

Finally, even when we have taken every cautious step to be as objective as we possibly could, we understand that someone is not going to agree with the price guides stated in this book. Those who overpaid for an identical or similar piece might believe that we did not know what we were doing, while those who have undersold another piece might suspect that we overstated the price for whatever reason(s). On the other hand, for every seller who undersells or a buyer who overpays for an item and does not agree with our estimated value, there is a buyer who gets a good buy or a seller who makes a good sale and feels great about such a transaction. Therefore, we shall leave those judgments to them. We also bear in mind that many collectors like to discount the values of the items given in any price guide. One of our customers once brought in a majolica book and pointed out to us that she would not pay more than sixty-six percent of the book value for any item listed in the book, and asked us to give her a thirty percent discount on an Etruscan Seaweed & Shell compote. We didn't agree. So we try not to inflate the values in this guide by assuming that they will be discounted by readers. Instead, we simply put down what our data shows, and shall let the readers make their own decisions.

Before we conclude this section, we would like to point out that all of the examples shown in this book were either owned by the author or by dealers and collectors. We did not use museum items because we try to avoid putting a price on any items that belong to a museum. However, this does not mean that the items in the museum are priceless. We simply prefer not to put a commercial value on any of them. On the other hand, many of the pieces that are illustrated in this book are of museum quality.

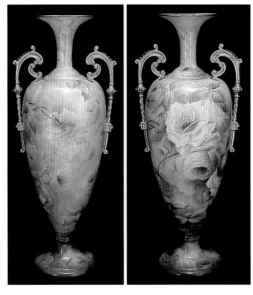

Figure 2. CAC/Lenox rose vase by artist, M.P. Heine, 18-1/2", sold at $2,500. *Photo and price are from courtesy of Laurel Antiques.*

Chapter 2
Ceramic Art Company and Lenox, Inc.™

Accomplished potters Jonathan Coxon and Walter Scott Lenox became co-workers at Ott and Brewer during the height of its Belleek years. With a loan of $4,000 from William Hancock, Coxon and Lenox went into a partnership in 1889 to form the Ceramic Art Company at Prince and Mead Street in Trenton, New Jersey. Coxon was the president and Lenox was the secretary, treasurer, and art director (Goldberg 1998, 52). They wasted no time in putting their rich Belleek experience to use for the realization of their own vision of Belleek making. They were good at both the overglazed and underglazed techniques.

In a few years, they had built a reputation as a maker of some of the finest decorative porcelains in the United States. Among the artists they hired, two very skillful artists, William W. Gallimore and Kate B. Sears, were especially important to the company. William W. Gallimore was a well-trained modeler who had worked in the Irish Belleek Works and Trent tiles. He designed a lot of their important pieces (Robinson, 38). The works of Kate B. Sears were especially noted for her unique way of decorating. She would use an ordinary jack-knife to carve the designs in the clay of the wares before burning. The elaborated decoration, entirely in relief, would come out crisp and beautiful (Barber 1893, 237). During that period, experiments with different ways of decorating were encouraged and new patterns constantly appeared in the company's decorated and undecorated wares. Lenox continued to put out a wide variety of delicate Belleek wares until the 1930s.

In 1895 Walter S. Lenox was unfortunately stricken with a sickness that eventually left him blind and paralyzed. Coxon, after leaving an indelible mark on the company, resigned from his post around 1896. Lenox, unwavering and dedicated, worked tirelessly despite his illness. Under his leadership, and with good potters at his side, the company continued to grow. By 1897 the company's catalog listed as many as 300 different items available for the public. By the end of the Ceramic Art Company period, they were known to be producing about 600 different shapes and patterns, with the emphasis on giftware. By WWII the company was offering more than 3,000 shapes with thousands of designs (Robinson, 75).

Walter Scott Lenox was born in Trenton, New Jersey, in 1859. His father owned a hardware business. As a young boy, Walter was not interested in hardware but was fascinated by pottery making. He served his apprenticeship at the Ott & Brewer factory at a very young age and became its art department head. He learned to be a sculptor as well as a decorator. After Ott & Brewer, he worked for Willets for a very short time. With Jonathan Coxon he formed the Ceramic Art Company in 1889. In 1895 he was afflicted with locomotor ataxia, which gradually left him blind and paralyzed. With the help of Harry Brown, his corporate secretary, and Frank Holmes, his chief designer, Lenox remained as the helmsman of the company until his death in 1920. Though never married, Walter Lenox enjoyed a rather flamboyant lifestyle. Charming and sociable, he was a frequent guest of many fine homes in New York and Philadelphia society. Being a well-respected citizen, he was always invited to lead parades in Trenton. He was known as someone who would do anything to keep his company going. Even sickness did not stop him, nor did financial hardship. Often, he would borrow money from friends to meet company expenses (Robinson 41).

As Walter Scott Lenox was going blind, his vision for the company had never been clearer, and that was for it to survive and prosper long after he was gone. Around 1900, he made two very important decisions that had great impact on the success of the company. One was to expand the product line to tableware; the other was to hire Frank Graham Holmes to replace him as the chief designer.

The expansion of tableware was mainly based on a new bone china formula developed by Charles Fergus Binns for dinnerware at Lenox. Charles Fergus Binns was a son of Richard W. Binns, who was the director of the Worcester Royal Porcelain Company. In 1902, a new product called Lenox China was introduced to the market. This new bone china was initially decorated by the same artists who used to decorate the art wares. Each service ware was individually designed and decorated. Most service wares were made to order, and highly trained enamellers and gilders would put on exquisite borders and monograms as required by customers. As it gradually achieved popularity, Walter S. Lenox expanded the line to include whole table services in stock patterns. By 1906 this line was so successful that the company changed its name to Lenox China and continued to offer exclusive designs and decorations for its rich customers (Venable, 140).

Another important decision Walter Lenox made was to hire Frank Graham Holmes as chief designer in 1905. Holmes held this job until his death in 1954. Born in Pawtucket, Rhode Island, in 1878, Holmes learned silver designs as an apprentice before he studied at the Rhode Island School of Design and the New York School of Art. He went back to work for a few silver companies before he joined Lenox. He created at least four hundred patterns from classical to modern designs for the company to accommodate the needs of different customers. He was awarded many important medals. One of Holmes' most important accomplishments was his appointment to design three sets of White House China: those for Woodrow Wilson in 1918, Franklin D. Roosevelt in 1934, and Harry S. Truman in 1951. Before the Wilson commission, all White House china wares were imported from abroad. It was generally believed then that American-made china wares were not as good as the foreign made ones. After the commission, Lenox china services were requested by heads of state around the world. Holmes was also appointed by the Secretary of Commerce Herbert Hoover to a Commission that reported on the International Exposition of Modern Decorative and Industrial Arts in Paris in 1925.

In 1906, the company name was officially changed to Lenox, and it began its most interesting and challenging times, times that would test its management tremendously. In the years that followed, while Walter Lenox's physical condition deteriorated, his spirit and ambition certainly did not. The company survived two world wars, depression, technology changes, numerous strikes, and many economic crises by constantly adjusting its products to fit the market. Dinnerware production was expanded greatly and transfer decorating was used instead of hand painting methods. By the end of World War I, two years before his death, an overdue accolade finally came to Walter Lenox and his peers. In March 1918 President Wilson chose Lenox service wares to grace the table of the White House. (Klaptbor 1975, 151).

In 1908, Lenox first dinnerware catalog offered a large variety of decorations of gold etchings, monograms, and fish game designs that the customers could order on their dinnerware. All of the dinnerware illustrated in the catalog was designed by Holmes.

From 1910 to 1920, porcelain decorating became one of the favorite pastimes in America. A lot of Lenox china blanks were decorated outside the factory by amateurs, hobbyists, and other studio artists. It was also trendy for silver manufacturers to put silver overlays on china blanks. It was during this period that Frank Holmes created his most innovative works, designs that made him famous. Throughout his career in Lenox he constantly had an innovative approach to respond to the needs of the market and the needs for the company's growth. When stock patterns were required, he designed printed-and-filled patterns such as The Virginian in 1910. When decal decoration was preferred, he designed Ming and Mandarin in 1917. His other major designs in this period were Mt. Vernon in 1911, Autumn in 1919, Maryland,

Coronado, and Florida in 1922, Pasadena and Fountain in 1926, and Washington-Wakefield in 1927 (Venable, 339).

By 1930, Lenox China, like many other companies, struggled to stay afloat during the Great Depression. To sustain growth, it diversified its business by producing porcelain items for other industries, such as lamp bases for the lighting industry, china inserts for silver companies, perfume bottles and atomizers for DeVilbiss, and X-ray spools and transformer shields for Westinghouse. In order to reduce costs, especially management costs, the executives took large pay cuts while the workforce took smaller ones. To cut production costs, more and more low-relief modeling tableware was produced instead of the costly gilding and colored decals. Fortunately, several factors worked favorably to the industry climate. In the 1930s, growing political instability in Europe curtailed the availability of foreign goods. A "Buy American" campaign was gaining ground at home. In addition, there was a change of consumer taste to a more simple and functional style. This change might be attributed to the influence of the Bauhaus thought. During this decade, as the Bauhaus ideology took hold of the design scene in Europe, it also quickly influenced design in America. Bauhaus Design School was founded in 1919 in Weimar, Berlin. Its theory stressed *the role of form in relation to function,* and that good design *"practice was not really cold functionalism but a balancing of function, aesthetics and technics to supply a commercial demand"* (Atterbury 1982, 221). In 1930, the State Porcelain Manufacturer of Berlin had conducted a survey in which 150 cups from museums were shown to the consumer public. The results found that consumers preferred a simple white cup made in 1750. In 1934, The Museum of Modern Art in New York held an exhibition of "Machine Art" in which some Lenox's tableware had the privilege of being chosen for display. It included some plain white porcelain plates and an absolutely cylindrical porcelain vase. In explaining the choices, *Barr, the museum's director, invoked Plato's dictum that geometrical shapes have absolute rather than relative beauty. "The most important aesthetic constituent of the machine product is the character of the material out of which it is made: in the case of porcelain, strength, delicacy, whiteness and translucency...form which is indicated by function, and which possesses the best attributes of machine manufacture—precision and quality material—will be beautiful in a more lasting way than anything produced in response to the dictates of fashion or apathy which ignores these qualities."* (Atterbury 1982, 222) Under these influences and the demand of the market for a cheaper product, Holmes designed Terrace and Three Step in 1932, and Beltane in 1936. All of these patterns depended on relief-molded rims to carry the design to cut cost in decorating. Other patterns by Holmes at this time were

Lenox Rose in 1934, Rhodora and Rutledge in 1939, and Harvest in 1940. A white cylindrical vase (Plate 176), made from 1930 to 1940, is shown to illustrate the style in that period, although it was not the one displayed at the exhibition of "Machine Art" in 1934.

Following World War II, in order to appeal to a broad cross section of consumers who could not afford expensive tablewares, the company made many changes. In 1947, with the help of Holmes, the director of manufacturing, John Tassie, drastically reduced its four hundred patterns to forty-seven in an effort to streamline production. The majority of patterns that survived this cut were designed by Holmes from 1932 to 1942. In the same year, dealer exclusivity was also eliminated. Before the change, some exclusive patterns were only available at certain expensive stores like Tiffany & Co. or Marshall Field & Co. After the change, all retailers who carried Lenox could order the same patterns. This greatly expanded the company's access to consumers. The number of retailers that handled Lenox wares had increased from 250 in 1938 to 767 in 1950. Since exclusive patterns were made in small numbers, it resulted in higher production cost. By eliminating this policy, production of the same pattern became more cost effective. With the increase in production and the decrease of skilled operations in the plant, quality control became inconsistent. To overcome that deficiency, Holmes designed Westwind in 1953 by spreading the pattern asymmetrically across the plate to give a broader coverage such that any escaped flaws in the ceramic body might be covered. (Venable 2000)

Throughout his long tenure with Lenox, Holmes proved to be an accomplished artist with boundless creativity. He was flexible in adapting to the needs of the market, yet never at the expense of elegant style or good taste. With his traditional art training and high fashion sense, he defined design of American dinnerware during his entire career. More importantly, he had good business sense and an effective leadership style. This can be summed up in one of his answers when asked about the success of his designs: "*I have often been asked how we know a new decoration will sell. We do not know. In most cases, we take a sporting chance...and we seldom mention failures.*" (Venable 2000)

Winslow Anderson took over the design department after Holmes's death in 1954. One of the most successful designs by Anderson was Kingsley. It was introduced in 1954, and like Ming and Autumn, it became one of the company's all time best-sellers. Around the same time, on the manufacturing side, John Tassie had simplified the table service wares and made the five-place setting standard for Lenox. With the popularity of Bridal registry, it made a table setting more affordable. For market research, Tassie would send people from his design department to interview women who were shopping in de-

partment stores. Sample patterns were shown to these shoppers and their preferences would be recorded for future references.

The 1950s were also the years when vigorous advertising paid off. Before 1940 Lenox only advertised its products to dealers. By 1950, it changed its target and advertised in almost all major home furnishing and teenager magazines to bring the company and its products directly to consumers. In that year, the company's advertising budget was 400 percent larger than that of its closest competitor. The advertising agency Phyllis Condon of D'Arcy took over the Lenox account in 1955 and created a slogan: "*You get the license...I'll get the Lenox*". (Venable, 143). This campaign lasted for nine years and was so successful that many still remember it, decades later. Yet the most imaginative campaign was the National Table Setting contest, which lasted from 1955 to 1983. Contestants were students from ninth grade and higher. They would submit a drawing of a table setting with noted choices for crystal, silver, and Lenox china together with a swatch of cloth for table linens. Their teachers would then select the best table settings and submit them to Lenox. From the entries, the company would choose three to four hundred "candidates" and present them to a panel of judges composed of well-known lifestyle personalities at the time. The winner's table setting would be featured in Bride's magazine. In the 1960s contests, they typically included three hundred thousand students from ten thousand schools. With this brand recognition, it is no wonder that in 1960, Lenox China could claim sixty percent of the fine china market in the United States while a lot of other U. S. potteries succumbed to foreign and domestic competition. (Venable 2000).

The company never stopped putting out new designs. In 1963, Oxford, a white bone china, was introduced but was discontinued in the late 1970s. Temperware, a more casual stoneware with emphasis on durability, was introduced in 1972, but it was eventually phased out in the 1980s. Chinastone, another casual ware with refined features to replace Temperware, came out in 1985 and is still being made.

In the 1970s Noritake, a Japanese company, took away some of Lenox 's market share by offering competitive quality for a cheaper price. In the fourth quarter of 1981, Noritake had 33.2 percent of the total dollar market share while Lenox had 20.7 percent. By 1991 the two companies were almost even in market share. By the end of 1998 Lenox's dollar market share of department store sales was 42 percent, more than twice that of Noritake and four times that of Josiah Wedgwood & Sons, an English company. (Venable 2000).

Until 1954 all Lenox china was made in Trenton, New Jersey. As expansion was required, a new factory was built in Pomona, New Jersey, near Atlantic City, where natural gas and water were abundant. Manufacturing continued in Trenton until 1964. During the 1980s, two more factories were built in North Carolina. Today this company, still based in New Jersey, put out a variety of gift related products, with a lot of them made in other countries.

Marks for CAC/Lenox

Most American Belleek pieces were marked, especially those made by both Ceramic Art Company-Lenox and Ott & Brewer. We found that Willets had the most unmarked items sold in the market, which was due to its lax quality control. Even many factory-decorated items were not marked. We tried to identify the date of each mark, and they are dated to the best of our knowledge. However, there might still be small discrepancies. For example, in most books and articles written by other authors, almost everyone mentioned that Mark 11 was used from 1906 to 1930. However, Lenox Rose (Mark 14) was

introduced in 1934 (pattern number code J300). Thus we believe that Mark 11 was used beyond 1930 and dated it to 1934. In our opinion, in collecting American Belleek, the precise date of an item that was made is not nearly so important, especially for those with gold marks. We have discussed the importance of age separately in this book. Since this book is mainly on American Belleek, we dated all those marks that were used after 1960 as new marks without elaboration, except Mark 16, which we believe was used from 1950 to 1955.

Mark 1. CAC wreath mark in red, lavender, brown, green, blue, or black used before 1896.

Mark 2. CAC Palette, with or without BELLEEK, in red, lavender, or green used from 1889 to 1896. Note the letters CAC have a different font from Marks 3 and 4. Here the word BELLEEK was replaced with a store name.

Mark 3. CAC Palette with BELLEEK in red, lavender, brown, blue, green, or black used from 1889 to 1906.

Mark 4. Same as Mark 3 except this one is in pink.

Mark 5. CAC Palette without BELLEEK in red and lavender used from 1889 to 1906. It might have other colors but we cannot confirm it. Here the word BELLEEK was replaced with a store name.

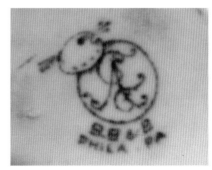

Mark 6. CAC with LENOX underneath wreath in pink, lavender, green, or gold (rare) used from 1896 to 1906. It is also called the "Transitional Mark".

Mark 7. CAC with LENOX underneath wreath in lavender, green, or gold (rare) used from 1896 to 1906. It is also called the "Transitional Mark". Note that the design of wreath in here is different from that of Mark 5.

Mark 8. Lenox Palette mark with initial "L" and BELLEEK usually in green used from 1906 to 1924 mainly on white wares sold to amateurs.

Mark 9. Lenox Palette mark with initial "L" but without BELLEEK usually in green, used after 1926 and most likely before 1930. It was used mainly on white wares and sold to amateurs.

Mark 10. Lenox Wreath mark with initial "L" and "DESIGN PATENT APPLIED FOR" in brown (rare color) that looks like gold used from 1906 to 1930.

Mark 11. Lenox Wreath mark with initial "L" in green used from 1906 to 1930. Note that the ribbon is different from others and it was used mainly in earlier years.

Mark 12. Lenox Wreath mark with initial "L" mainly in green and occasionally in other colors (such as black, pink, blue, and gold (very rare)) used from 1906 to 1934.

Mark 13. Lenox Wreath mark with initial "L" and "SILVER LENOX" underneath wreath in green used from 1925 to 1926 (?).

Mark 14. Lenox Wreath mark with initial "L" mainly in green and occasionally in other colors (such as black, pink, blue, and gold (very rare)) used from 1906 to 1934. It usually had a pattern name such as MING or Monticello below it and sometimes also came with the words "pattern design applied for".

Mark 15. Lenox Wreath mark with initial "L" mainly in green and occasionally in other colors (such as black, pink, and blue) used from 1906 to 1934. Sometimes it came with the pattern name.

Mark 16. Lenox Wreath mark with initial "L" and "Made in USA" underneath wreath, mainly in green and occasionally in other colors (such as black, pink, and blue) used from 1930 to late 1940s. Note that the words "Made in USA" are in straight line, which is older than the mark with "Made in USA" in curved line.

Mark 17. Lenox Wreath mark with initial "L", "BY LENOX", and "Made in USA" in a curved line underneath the wreath in gold, c. 1950 to 1955.

Mark 18. Lenox Wreath mark with initial "L" and "Made in USA" in curved shape underneath wreath, mainly in green and gold, used from 1978 to present. Note that the words "Made in USA" are in a curved line, which represents a newer mark than those in a straight line (Mark 15.)

Mark 19. Same as Mark 18 except this one is in the gold color.

Mark 20. Lenox Wreath mark with initial "L", "LENOX", and "Made in USA" in a curved line underneath the wreath in gold. New mark.

Mark 21. Lenox Wreath mark with initial "L", "LENOX", and "Made in USA" in a curved line underneath the wreath in gold. New mark.

Mark 22. Lenox Wreath mark with initial "L", "LENOX", and "Made in USA" in a curved line underneath the wreath in gold. New mark.

Mark 23. Lenox Wreath mark with initial "L", "LENOX", and "Made in USA" in a curved line underneath the wreath in gold. New mark.

Mark 24. Lenox Wreath mark with initial "L", "LENOX", and "Made in USA" in a curved line underneath the wreath in gold. New mark.

Plates 1 and 2. Classical shape vase, factory hand-painted with tea roses on an apple green ground and decorated with gilded designs on its back. Although unsigned, it was attributed to George Morley. See Plates 4 to 6 to compare the painting techniques and rose styles with those on the inkwell, which was decorated and signed by George Morley. Mark 7, 10", $650-850.

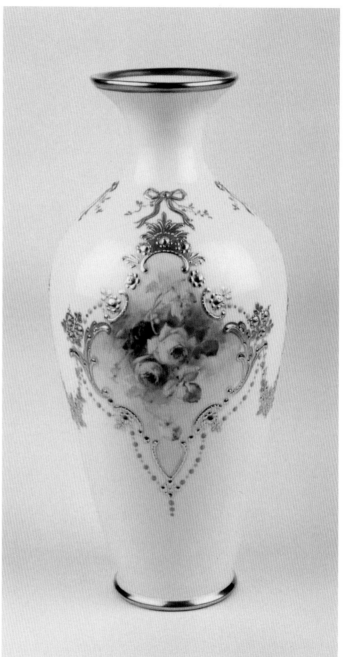

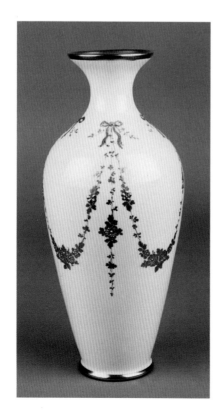

Plates 4, 5, 6. Inkwell, decorated with tea roses and leaves on an apple green ground by George Morley and signed. Mark 7, 3-1/2" x 3-1/2", $425-475.

Plate 3. Details of decoration of vase in Plates 1 and 2.

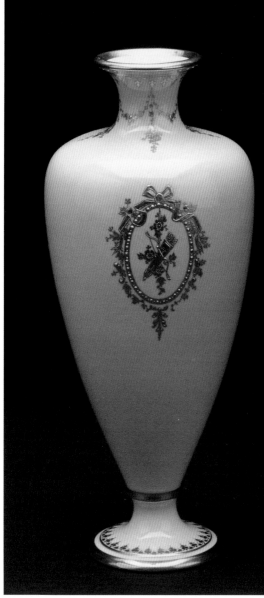

Plate 10. Detail of decoration of vase attributed to H. J. Nosek.

Plate 11. Cylindrical vase, factory hand-painted with rose buds, leaves, and rose on a white ground by Han John Nosek and signed J. Nosek. This was one of Nosek's *last works* at Lenox. Mark 17, 12", $650-850.

Opposite page:
Plates 7, 8, 9. Classical shape vase, factory hand-painted with an eighteenth century lady on an apple green ground and decorated with gilded designs on its back. Although unsigned, it was attributed to Han John Nosek, and is considered one of his best works at Lenox. Mark 7, 12-1/2" x 5", $1,500-2,000.

Plate 12. Bulbous vase, factory hand-decorated with white water lilies and leaves in a pond on both sides by George Morley and signed; unusual decoration. Mark 12, 7-1/4" x 6-1/4", $750-850.

Plate 14. Fine cabinet vase, factory hand-painted with bouquets of flowers and gold impasto on both sides by Walter Marsh and signed Marsh. Cabinet vases are considered rare and highly desirable especially signed by renowned artists. This is one example where size may not affect its value as a smaller item may be priced higher than a larger one. Mark 3, 4", $300-400.

Plate 13. The other side of the George Morley vase shown in Plate 12.

Plate 15. The other side of Plate 14.

Plate 16. Two-handle vase, factory hand-painted with roses and leaves by George Morley and signed. Mark 16, 7" x 8-1/2", $650-750.

We can study the differences in techniques, shapes of flowers and leaves, and colors applied to find out how the four famous artists (H. J. Nosek, Walter Marsh, George and William Morley) painted roses and leaves. Although Marsh (Plates 258 & 261) and the Morleys used turquoise color to highlight the shadows of leaves, Marsh used the most while George (Plates 16 & 19) used the least (he used more green and yellow) and William (Plates 17 & 18) fell in the middle. Nosek (Plates 11 & 21) did not use any at all. Nosek painted the roses and leaves with great details while George used simple strokes to express his art, and the other two fell somewhere in between. Each one had his own flower style and leaf shapes too. Although Marsh used two different styles to paint roses, the colors (turquoise mixed with brown and yellow ochre) used on the leaves were quite consistent. The colors of roses are also slightly different.

Plates 17 and 18. Flaring vases, factory hand-painted with roses and leaves by William Morley, one signed. This pair was featured in the Robinson & Feeny Price Guide and is both their and our favorite. Mark 12, 5-3/4", $800-1,000 a pair or $300-400 if sold separately. An example of a pair or set is priced higher than the sum of individual piece.

Plate 19. Large flaring vases, factory hand-painted with roses and leaves by George Morley and signed. Mark 16, 10-1/4" x 9", $650-850.

Plate 20. Cider pitcher, professional hand decoration with roses and leaves on both sides, signed M. Robinson and dated Nov. 1902. Mark 3, 5-1/2" x 7-1/2", $350-400.

Plate 21. Large flaring vase, factory hand-painted with yellow tea roses and leaves by Han John Nosek and signed. Mark 16, 10-3/4" x 8", $900-1,000.

Plate 22. The other side of Plate 20.

Plate 23. Cup and saucer set, factory hand-painted with roses and leaves. Although unsigned, these were attributed to William Morley and were often referred to as Morley Rose cups and saucers by most collectors and by Robinson and Feeny. Mark 7, cup 2-1/2", saucer 5-1/4", $125-175 each set.

Plate 24. Details of bowls on Plate 25.

Plate 25. Bowls, with hand-decorated roses, gilded designs, and gold scallop rim. Mark 7 and Tiffany mark, 2" H x 3-1/4" D, $150-250 each.

Plate 26. Bowl with factory hand-painted flowers and green exterior. Mark 7, 2" H x 4" D, $125-150.

Plates 27 and 28. Morley plates, hand-painted orchids and surrounded by an acid-etched gilt border inside an ivory band. Morley plates with orchid are among the most desirable American Belleek and far more desirable than with game birds and fish decorations. Mark 12, 8-1/2", $350-450 each or $5,000-6,000 set of 12.

Plate 29. Same as Plates 27 and 28.

Plate 30. Same as Plates 27 and 28.

Plate 31. Same as Plates 27 and 28.

Plate 32. Same as Plates 27 and 28.

Plate 33. Morley plate, hand-painted fish (Yellow Perch) and surrounded by an acid-etched gilt border. Mark 12, 9-1/2", $200-250 each or $3,000-3,500 set of 12.

Plate 34. Same as Plate 33, except this plate was painted with Sun Fish.

Plate 35. Morley plate, hand-painted game bird and surrounded by a heavy, acid-etched gilt border with monogram HWS. The large gilded border constitutes a higher price, which was offset by the monogram. Mark 12, 9", $325-375 each or $4,250-4,750 set of 12.

Plate 36. Same as Plate 35.

Plate 37. Same as Plate 35.

Plate 38. Same as Plate 35.

Plate 39. Same as Plate 35.

Plates 40 and 41. Coffee pot, factory hand-painted with Oncidium Orchids and gilded accents. Mark 6, 10-1/2", $425-525.

Plate 42. Center bowl, professionally painted with roses and leaves and with gilded rim and handles. Mark 8, 12-1/4" L x 5" H, $275-325.

Plate 43. The other side of Plate 44.

Plate 44. Factory hand-painted tankard with grapes on both sides. Mark 8, 7-1/4", $175-225.

Plate 45. Pitcher, factory-decorated with gilt-painted flowers and leaves. Gilt-painted items were almost always factory-decorated and the artworks were usually superb. They are currently under priced but have great potential. They go very well with any collections. Mark 4 (in black), 4", $135-175.

Plate 46. Set of eight ramekins, factory hand-painted with flowers.
Mark 5, 1-1/4" H x 3-3/8" D, $50-65 each or $400-500 set of 8.

Plate 47. Pitcher, factory-decorated with holly
leaves and berries. Mark 7, 5-1/4" x 4-1/2",
$150-200.

Plate 48. Pitcher, factory-decorated with flowers,
leaves, and enamels on a pearl-like glaze; small nick
to spout. Mark 5, 4" H x 3-1/2", $150-200.

Plate 49. Liners with sterling silver holders by Mauser. All Mauser liners were factory hand-painted with flowers and have apple green exterior. Mauser sets do not come with saucers. Mark 6 for liners, 2" H, silver holders have slightly different sizes and marked Mauser, 2-3/4" approx., $200-250 each.

Plate 50. Details of liners for Plate 49.

Plate 51. Bowls, factory hand-painted with flowers and gold bows. Exterior has light rainbow color tint. Mark 6, 3" H x 4" D, $150-175.

Plate 52. Rare Chocolate cup liners, factory hand-painted with flowers in great details and heavy gold accents. One with Mark 7 and one with Mark 12 indicating that they were made in 1906, 3" H , $150-175 each.

Plate 53. Details of Plate 52.

Plate 54. Set of 12 Chocolate cup liners, factory hand-decorated with blue enamel dots and gilded details. Many different items can be found in this popular pattern. Mark 7, 3" H, $65-95 each.

Plate 55. RARE doorknobs, factory hand-decorated with floral patterns. Doorknobs were unmarked and can only be identified through both shapes and decorations. They are very desirable to collectors. 2-1/2", $275-350 each.

Plate 56. Set of 6 cup liners with sterling silver holders and saucers. Cup liners with sterling sets are way under priced with so many pieces available in the market, prices may not go up as fast as other items. They make great wedding presents, just like they used to. Liners with Mark 12, 2" H (without holder), holders 2" H, saucers with monogram 3-3/4" D, $35-45 each or $210-240 set of 6.

Plate 57. Pair of cup liners with sterling silver holders and saucers. Liners with Mark 7, 1-1/2" H, holder 1-1/2" H, saucer 3", $35-45 each.

Plate 58. Cup liner with solid sterling silver holder and saucer. Liners with Mark 12, 2" H, holder 2-1/8" H, saucer 3-3/4", $45-50 each.

Plate 59. Set of 6 liners in rare cobalt blue. Colored liners are more like glass and chip easily, but are highly sought after by collectors. Two with small flecks, Mark 7, 2-1/4" H, $250-300 set of 6.

Plate 60. Different sizes of liners; smallest 1-1/2" H, largest (chocolate) 3" H.

Plate 61. Pair of cup liners with sterling silver holders and saucers. Liners with Mark 12, 2" H, holder 2-1/2" H, saucer 3-1/4", $45-50 each.

Plate 62. Pair of cup liners with sterling silver holders with monogram MOM. Liners with Mark 12, 2" H, holder 2-1/4" H, $30-35 each.

Plate 63. Platter with wide 4" sterling rim, pattern of the 8" porcelain plate is Grenoble. It was first introduced in 1930. Items with sterling rim or overlay are better investment than liners with holders as they are much more difficult to find. Mark 10, overall size 16", $350-400.

Plate 64. Brown pitcher with silver overlay, rare color. Mark 12, 5-1/2", $175-200.

Plate 65. White pitcher with silver overlay, Mark 12, 5-1/2", $125-150.

Plate 66. Cup and saucer set with silver overlay in floral design. Mark 12, cup 1-3/4" H, saucer 5" D, $150-200 each set.

Plate 67. Plate with sterling rim, pattern of porcelain plate, Peachtree, was first introduced in 1948. Mark 19, 9-1/2", $200-225.

Plate 68. Plate with extensive silver overlay. Mark 9, 9-1/2", $225-275.

Plate 69. Sugar and creamer with silver overlay, cobalt color on both. Mark 12, sugar 3-1/2", creamer with crack to rim 4" H, $150-200.

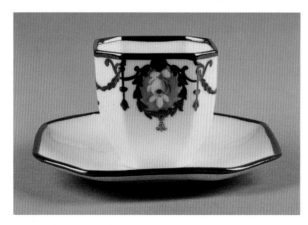

Plate 72. Sugar bowl with silver overlay and hand-painted flower. Mark 8, 4-1/4" H x 5-1/2", $150-175.

Plates 70 and 71. Cup and saucer with silver overlay, cup has hand-painted flower. Mark 8, cup 2-1/8", saucer 4-1/2", $150-175.

Plate 73. Cabinet vase with silver overlay in rare light blue color. Porcelain vases are usually large and cabinet vases, especially with silver overlay, are very scarce. Also light blue (not cobalt) color is extremely hard to find and this vase, that has all three rarities in one item, is a real gem. Mark 7, 3-3/4", $400-500.

Plate 75. Platter with sterling rim, pattern of porcelain plate, Aurora, was first introduced in 1936. Mark 16, overall size 11-1/2", $275-325.

Plate 74. Soup bowl with saucer set, pattern Synthia was first introduced in 1939. Mark 16, Soup bowl 2", saucer 6-1/4", $30-40.

Plate 76. Virginian bread plate with monogram. See detailed description on Plate 78. Mark 12, 5-3/4", $100-125 each.

Plate 77. Rare Virginian cover muffin dish without monogram. See detailed description on Plate 78. Mark 12, 3" H x 7-1/4" D, $400-500.

Plate 78. Dinner plate with Virginian pattern without monogram. Mark 12, 10-1/2", $250-300 each.

Virginian pattern was one of the first patterns introduced by Lenox to expand its service wares market in 1910. Instead of selling its products in an all hand-painted way, it was a new approach by using transfer-print to set the outlines and hand-painted inside the outlines for details. It has rose baskets, country landscape, and portrait medallions in addition to hand-applied enamels and gilded patterns. Although they have transfer-print outlines, each piece looks slightly different from the others because of its hand-painted decoration. Such new methods reduced the workload of the busy artists by assigning most hand painting works to designers and increased production capacity. Since every piece still required intensive labor, the costs of production were high. Naturally they were sold mainly to the more wealthy. Thus, most of the Virginian pieces were also monogrammed and sold in expensive department stores. Even today, they remain the most expensive pieces in the service ware categories except those earlier pieces with all hand-painted decorations such as the Morley plates. Although this new method of transfer-print and hand-fill-in painting proved to be successful, this particular pattern was too expensive to produce and the market was limited. So Lenox began to introduce other designs that required less work such as the Mount Vernon in 1911 (also nicknamed as the poor man's Virginian), Tuxedo in 1912, Meadowbrook and Windsor in 1915, Stanford in 1916, and Mandarin and Ming in 1917. Because of high prices, relatively few pieces of Virginian were sold then; they are quite hard to find in the current market as well and they represent a certain prestige in any collection.

Plate 79. Virginian coffee cup and saucer sets with monogram. See detailed description on Plate 78. Mark 12, cup 2-1/2" H, saucer 6-1/8" D, $175-225 each.

Plate 80. Virginian teacup and saucer sets with monogram. See detailed description on Plate 78. Mark 12, cup 2-1/4" H, saucer 5-1/2" D, $175-225 each.

Plate 81. Different in sizes of coffee and teacups and saucers.

Plate 82. Virginian sugar and creamer set with monogram. See detailed description on Plate 78. Mark 12, sugar 4-1/4" H, creamer 3" H, $300-350 set.

Plate 83. RARE Virginian eggcup and saucer set with monogram. See detailed description on Plate 78. Mark 12, eggcup 3-3/4" H, saucer 5-1/2" D, $175-225 set.

Plate 84. Sauce dish, factory hand-painted with flowers and gilded accents. Mark 12, 4-1/4" D, $45-55.

Plate 86. Mayonnaise bowl with underplate, Mt. Vernon pattern. Although Mayonnaise has its own underplate (shape #1180), many collectors use a 7" plate as its underplate. Complete set is hard to find. Mark 12, bowl 3-1/8" H x 5" D, underplate 6-3/8", $225-275; if with a 7" plate, $175-225.

Plate 85. Tea Caddy, Mount Vernon pattern. Mark 12, 5" H, $225-275.

Although Mt. Vernon was nicknamed "a poor man's Virginian," and most of them were not monogramed, it was indeed very finely decorated with floral baskets and hand-applied enamels, and was heavily gilded. It was among the better patterns produced by Lenox.

Plate 87. Footed cup, Mt. Vernon pattern; never came with a saucer. Mark 12, 2-5/8", $65-85.

Plate 88. Sugar bowl and creamer, Mt. Vernon pattern. Sugar bowl was an open one without lid. Mark 12, sugar bowl 4" H x 6-1/4", creamer 5-1/2" H, $250-300 set.

Plate 89. Sugar bowl and creamer, finely painted with flowers and leaves on an apple green ground with unusual handle to creamer. Wear to gilded area. Mark 8, sugar bowl 4" D, creamer 4-1/2" H, $300-350 set.

Plate 90. Dinner plate, Monticello pattern, first introduced in 1928. Its quality is better than both Mandarin and Ming, although Ming lasted much longer for almost 50 years. Mark 14, 10-1/2", $55-65 each.

Plate 91. Bread plate: the Mandarin pattern, first introduced in 1917, was a sister pattern of Ming, except it had better quality and was more expensive to produce; so it did not last as long as Ming during the Great Depression. For the same reason, it is a better collectible than Ming today. Mark 12, 6-1/4", $12-15 each.

Plate 92. Cup and saucer set, Lenox Rose pattern, decorated with transfer-print of roses and was first introduced in 1934. This pattern lasted over 40 years and the supply is plentiful in the market today. So many collectors prefer only those with the pink mark made in the early years. Mark 15 in pink, cup 2-1/8" H, saucer 5-5/8", $50-60; marks in other colors $30-35 with gold marks or green marks with only words of Lenox Rose in pink.

Plate 93. Cup and saucer set, Mandarin pattern, first introduced in 1917 with transfer-print and hand enhanced decoration. Mark 12, cup 2-1/8", saucer 5-5/8", $30-35 a set.

Plate 94. Footed Plate with large monogram "C" and acid-etched gilt border. Monogram with single letter has minimum effect on price. Mark 12, 10-1/2", $175-225.

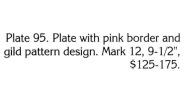

Plate 95. Plate with pink border and gild pattern design. Mark 12, 9-1/2", $125-175.

Plate 96. Plate with transfer-print and hand decoration of wild geese in flight. This was not a regular pattern and is more difficult to find today; small restoration to back. Mark 12, 9", $95-125 or $175-250 if mint.

Plate 97. Bread plate, Ming pattern, with transfer-print of Chinese style floral decoration in center and a border with birds in flight. Ming was first introduced in 1917 and lasted about 50 years. It is a very pleasant design with flowers, birds, and butterfly, and has a large variety of items. However, it has a problem of quality control and colors were inconsistent (see the two plates here) and fade easily. Over a half century, there was, and still is, a huge supply of these items in the market. Mark 14 in black, 7-1/4", $15-20 each.

Plate 98 and 99. Mayonnaise bowl with underplate, Ming pattern. Mayonnaise bowl is considered rare and very desirable. However, it is hard to find the original underplate and many collectors use the bread plate instead. Mark 14, bowl 3-1/8" H x 5" D, underplate 7-1/4", $100-125.

Plates 100 and 101. Cup and saucer set decorated with transfer-print of a motto from Shakespeare, "*See the Players Well Bestow'd*", the comedy and tragedy masks, and hand applied pink enamel. This is one of the better Commemorative items with wide appeal. Mark 4, cup 2-1/2", saucer 5", $250-300 a set.

Plates 102 and 103. Demitasse cup and saucer set decorated with transfer-print commemorating the banquet of the Crockery Broad of Trade of New York, 2/12/1897 at Delmonico's and hand applied turquoise enamels. This set is a good collectible for ceramic collectors. Mark 6, cup 1-1/2", saucer 4-1/2", $175-225 a set.

Plate 104. Plates with scalloped and gilded rim, factory hand-painted with grapes on transferred outlines by a noted artist, F. Fenzel, whose signature appears on one. Fenzel worked at Lenox from 1937-1946 when most of Lenox's products were with only print-transfer decoration without hand paintings. Hand-painted items in those years were considerably rare and are highly desirable. The two plates appear differently. Mark 16, 9-1/2", $200-250 each.

Plate 105. Plate with scalloped and gilded rim, factory hand-painted apples with transferred outlines by F. Fenzel and signed. Mark 16, 9-1/2", $200-250.

Plate 106. Plate with scalloped and gilded rim, and a wide green border. Mark 16, 9-1/2", $100-125.

Plates 107 and 108. Morley plates, decorated with hand-painted beautiful flowers and surrounded by a rare apple green border with gilded rim. Morley plates with flowers are less common than with game birds and fish decorations. For those who collect American Belleek with flowers, these kinds of floral plates are more desirable. Mark 12, 9", $250-300 each or $3,500-4,000 set of 12.

Plate 109. Same as Plates 107 and 108.

Plate 110. Same as Plates 107 and 108.

Plate 111. Same as Plates 107 and 108.

Plate 112. Same as Plates 107 and 108.

Plate 113. Same as Plate 114. Here it shows the metal mechanism that goes inside the jar.

Plates 114. Rare covered Potpourri Jar with a metal mechanism; factory hand-painted with beautiful roses and gilded leaves. The detailed gilded leaves enhance the beauty and add value to it. Mark 4, 5-1/4", $400-500.

Plate 115. Rare covered Potpourri Jar with a metal mechanism, factory hand-painted with Violets. Mark 4, 5-1/4", $300-400.

Plate 157. Flaring vase in rare burgundy with acid-etched decorations. Mark 12, 8-1/4" H x 7-1/4", $300-400.

Plate 158. Lenox dealer's sign, unmark, 4" x 3", $40-60.

Plate 159. Flaring vase in rare yellow color. Mark 12, 5-3/4" H x 5-1/4", $200-250.

Plates 160 and 161. Tall vase with two stylish handles, factory hand-painted with red, yellow, and pink tea roses and green leaves on a shaded pale yellow and green ground with gilded details. Mark 4, 19", $2,000-2,500.

Plates 162 and 163. Large and fine classically shaped vase, factory hand-painted with purple irises on a mottled green ground. Decoration of irises is less common than that of roses. The artist's work is exceptional. Mark 3, 15", $1,350-1,650.

Plate 164. See Plate 165 for details.

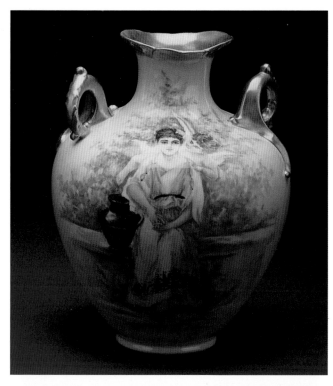

Plate 165. Bulbous urn, professionally hand-painted with women and cupids in neo-classical landscape. The paintings of a woman with cupids were inspired by a French artist, Adolphe-William Bouguereau (1825-1905). One of his oil paintings, "*Work Interrupted, 1891*", depicted a cupid in midair interrupting a lady's work of winding wool. The painting (65" x 40" approx.) is now in the collection of Mead Art Museum, Amherst College. This urn was signed A. G. Ward. Mark 4, 11" H x 9", $2,250-2,750.

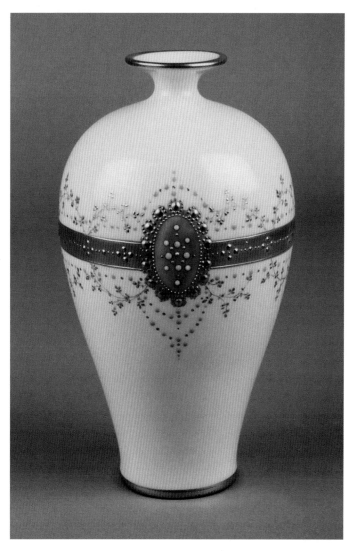

Plate 166. Covered bulbous jar, factory hand-gilded and enameled with sprigs, blue dots, and medallions in great details. Mark 12, 5-1/2" H x 5-1/2" D, $400-500.

Plate 167. Bulbous vase, factory hand-gilded and enameled with sprigs, blue dots, and medallions in great details. Mark 7, 7" H, $350-400.

Plate 168. Demitasse coffee pot, factory hand-decorated with turquoise enamel, blue dot garlands, and gold. Mark 16, 6" H, $250-300.

Plate 169. Demitasse tea or coffee pots, factory hand-decorated with turquoise enamel, blue dot garlands, and gold. Mark 16, 5" H, $250-300.

Plate 170. Demitasse tea or coffee pots, factory hand-decorated with turquoise enamel, blue dot garlands, and gold. Mark 16, 5" H, $250-300.

Plate 171. Large and unusual bowl, factory hand-decorated with fine Chinese dragons. This bowl was made specially for Bailey Banks & Biddle. Mark 11, 10-1/2" D x 3" H, $350-450.

Plate 173. Beehive honey pot, newer version. Mark 19, 5-1/2", $125-150.

Plate 172. Beehive honey pot with applied gold bees on the sides and one bee on its lid as its finial. Older ones have gold stripes on the pots. There is another version with silver lids and they are priced about the same. Mark 12, 5-1/2", $150-175.

Plate 174. Plates in Monroe pattern. Mark 21 for dinner plate, 10-1/2", $25-30; and Mark 24 for lunch/salad plate, 8-1/2", $15-20.

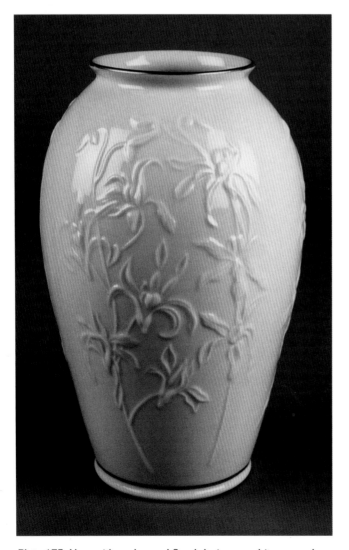

Plate 175. Vase with embossed floral design on white ground. Mark 20, 7-1/4", $35-40.

Plate 176. Cylindrical vase, embossed with a landscape in oriental style on a white ground. Mark 16, 9", $95-125.

Plate 177. Vase, embossed with arts & crafts design on white ground. Mark 19, 4-1/4" x 4-1/4", $30-40.

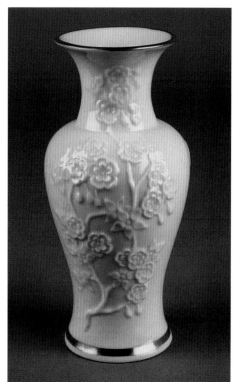

Plate 178. Vase, embossed with floral design on white ground. Mark 20, 6-1/4", $30-35.

Plate 179. Plates in Fresh Meadow pattern. Mark 22, dinner plate, 10-1/2", $30-35; lunch/salad plate, 8", $20-25.

Chapter 3
Ott & Brewer

In May of 1863, Joseph Ott, a native of Hunterdon County, New Jersey, went into a partnership with William Bloor and Thomas Booth under the name Bloor, Ott and Booth. They erected a pottery on Clinton Avenue on the outskirts of the city of Trenton. The pottery broke ground in May and, in November of the same year, it was reported that goods were turned out from the factory. It may be largely due to the fact that William Bloor was on the team. Born in England and trained as a potter there, Bloor was regarded as a significant force in promoting white ware in Trenton. As a result, white ware became the major output both in Ohio and in New Jersey. (Goldberg 1998, 29). This enabled a lot of potteries to prosper and allowed them to be in a position to engage in more ambitious work.

Thomas Booth retired from the pottery in 1864 and sold his interest to Garrett Burroughs. In July 1865, John Hart Brewer, Ott's twenty-one year old nephew, bought Burroughs's interest in the company. William Bloor, after helping to lay a good foundation and leave valuable expertise to his successors, retired from the pottery in 1871 (Goldberg 1998, 31). The so-called B. O. B. period could mean any of the three time frames: 1) Bloor, Ott and Booth from 1863 to 1864, 2) Bloor, Ott and Burroughs from 1864 to 1865, or 3) Bloor, Ott and Brewer from 1865 to 1871. It was not clear when the company mark changed to Ott & Brewer, but it should not be before 1871.

In the early years, decorated granite ware and cream colored wares were the main staples of the pottery. Herman Rolege, a major decorator in Trenton, worked on a lot of their granite wares. (Robinson, 334)

At the time of Bloor's departure, John Brewer, who worked alongside him for six years, was ready to take over the company's directorship. To expand the parian line, he hired Isaac Broom in 1875, who was a renowned American sculptor. In 1876, Ott & Brewer was able to put out a ware known as "ivory porcelain." It was regarded as the first entirely American made porcelain (Goldberg 1998, 31). It resembled Irish Belleek in style but not in composition, and it was not as fine. (Robinson, 334) In the 1876 Philadelphia Centennial Exhibition, Ott & Brewer displayed both their parian wares and this "ivory porcelain." The Company was awarded a medal for the finest display of parian ware and statuary wares. (History of Burlington and Mercer Counties)

In the same Exhibition, Irish Belleek made its official debut in America and caused such sensation that it probably overshadowed all of the American made porcelain in the show. For years the Trenton potters had been dreaming of making fine porcelain that could rival the Europeans. When they saw the superior quality of the Irish Belleek, they admired what the Irish potters were able to do and, at the same time, they believed they could do the same. To them the word "Belleek" became a symbol of fine porcelain at its best, in terms of artistic style, superior body texture, and glaze. John Brewer, being the perfectionist, harbored the same dream. In 1882 he sought the help of William Bromley, Jr. in experimenting with the production of Belleek wares. Not happy with the results, a year later he sought the help from William Bromley, Sr., whose expertise in Irish Belleek was more first hand. He was the manager of Mr. Goss, who was the inventor of the Irish Belleek china body (Barber 1893, 215). Around late 1883 or early 1884, Ott & Brewer successfully made the first American Belleek, a fine porcelain ware that resembled Irish Belleek but was made entirely from American materials with soil from the New Jersey clay beds and water from the Delaware River. It was a joint effort between the American potters and Irish potters who chose to call America their home and the place to pursue their careers.

One of the early pieces was described as a square tray, supported by four legs, white ground with a morning-glory design in blue and gold, and a scalloped rim outlined in gold (Reilly 1952). Plate 191 illustrates an example. A lot of Ott & Brewer's Belleek resembled that of Irish Belleek and Royal Worcester porcelain because many immigrant potters were associated with these two companies. Among them, the Bromleys from Irish Belleek Work were considered the major influence. Others, such as William Morris—who was trained at the Irish Belleek Work and in the Royal Worcester Porcelain Works, and F.R. Willmore—who worked in Royal Worcester, came to work for Ott & Brewer as a foreman and a decorator respectively. Later, these two men joined together to start their own pottery as Morris & Willmore, also known as the Columbian Art Pottery. Evolutions like this happened all the time in the industry. Potters would work together to make something happen. During the process they learned from each other, and then they would go their separate ways and compete with each other, challenging each other to improve, advance, and produce better products.

In the ten years of Belleek production, Ott & Brewer had not stopped improving the quality of its wares. Many regard their porcelain as the finest porcelain ever produced in the United States. In the 1889 Pottery and Glassware Exhibition at Memorial Hall in Philadelphia for the Encouragement of the Ceramic Arts, Ott & Brewer's display was so impressive that an article in the *Daily True American* said:

> ...they have advanced with steady progression to the enviable position of leaders in the fine art of pottery in this country, and have placed themselves on the front rank of all the potters of the world. It is true that their first efforts in this line were duplicates of the few pieces, then in this country, of the famous Irish Belleek, but a glance at their display in Philadelphia will convince anyone at all acquainted with the art that they have improved and beautified this class of goods to a wonderful extent...It is worthy of notice that the great house of Tiffany, in New York, has given an order for the entire display of Belleek goods as it now stands in the exhibition. This is more than an ordinary compliment, as it brings with it the substantial appreciation of one of the highest authorities in this country on fine modern porcelain. (*Daily True American*, October 30, 1889, Goldberg 1998, 32)

When compared to Irish Belleek, Ott & Brewer's Belleek had the same rich iridescence of the nacreous glaze, while the weight of their wares was even lighter than that of its Irish competitor. When their thinnest examples were picked to emphasize this quality, a dozen cups and saucers would weigh about one pound. (Barber 1893, 217).

Due to decline in demand of high quality products, Ott & Brewer was forced into suspension of production in 1892 and receiver's sale in 1893 (Goldberg 1998, 33).

John Hart Brewer and his contributions to his own pottery and to the Trenton pottery industry as a whole are best explained with this quote from the *Pottery and Glassware Reporter* of June 18, 1891:

> ...Mr. Brewer, like the early potters of the English and French schools, has been more interested in achieving practical success than in making money, and, as a consequence, is not as wealthy as some of his more conservative contemporaries. He has spent many thousand dollars in arriving at the present stage, and the American industry generally has shared in its benefits...The United States Potters' Association, which has done much to unify, strengthen, and advance the pottery interests of this country, was suggested and successfully organized by Mr. Brewer, who was for some years its secretary, and subsequently became its president. His familiar face is seen at every convention, and it is hard to tell when he is at his best, in the serious discussions of the convention, or when, as toastmaster at the banquet, the speakers are introduced with witty and appropriate remarks. In 1875 he was elected to the New Jersey House of Assembly in a district that usually went Democratic, and

subsequently became a Representative in both the 47th and 48th Congresses, where he speedily became recognized as one the most intelligent exponents and advocates of the tariff question, and gained a national reputation. Mr. Brewer is a thoroughly practical potter, familiar with all the details of the industry, acquainted with all its ups and downs during the past twenty-six years, and always taking an active interest in anything relating to its advancement. In the recent efforts to cultivate the spirit of practical art by offering prizes to the various art schools he has been prominent. His genial manners and kindly disposition have endeared him to all he has come in contact with, and even in the heat of political strife he has commanded the respect and friendship of his opponents. No employer is more popular among his employees, and no manufacturer more respected among his colleagues. Mr. Brewer was born in Hunterdon County, N.J., March 29, 1844, and is a lineal descendant, on his mother's side, of John Hart, one of the signers of the Declaration of Independence. (Barber 1893, 218-220)

When the company suspended its operations, Brewer was not yet fifty years old. For a short time, he helped out at the old Taylor and Speeler site, which produced sanitary ware. He also worked as the Assistant Appraiser of the Port of New York until his death in December of 1900.

At the 1901 Annual Convention of the U.S. Potters Association, his peers adopted a resolution as a tribute to him.

> Few, if any, have had the ability, opportunity or willingness to do what he did for the pottery industry of the United States. At the Centennial, the New Orleans and World's Fair exhibitions, by the product of his genius he revealed to our people the possibilities of our industry, in the halls of Congress he championed our cause, as Assistant Appraiser at the Port of New York, he protected our interests, and as president of this organization and chairman of many important committees he led our association to success at great and irreparable loss to himself. (Goldberg 1998)

According to Goldberg, Charles H. Cook acquired the Ott & Brewer plant in 1894. The new company, The Cook Pottery Company, kept producing pottery until the Great Depression when the plant was demolished in 1932.

Marks for Ott and Brewer

The business of producing American Belleek by Ott and Brewer lasted from 1883 to 1893. During these ten years, the company used a few marks for their products. Two of the marks (not shown in this book) were simply letter marks. The first one was OTT & BREWER CO. BELLEEK in the shape of a circle and the second mark was "MANUFACTURED BY-OTT & BREWER-TRENTON, NJ USA," and arranged in three lines. The other marks are illustrated below. All these marks were dated from 1883-1893.

Mark 1. Crescent mark with letters O & B, the word BELLEEK on top, TRENTON in the middle and NJ at the bottom.

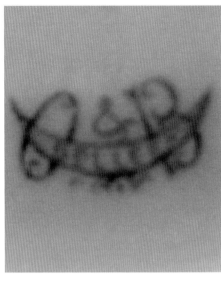

Mark 2. Crescent mark with the word BELLEEK inside the new moon.

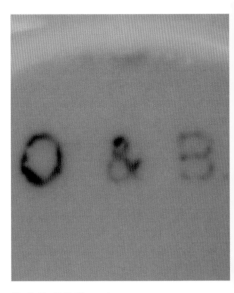

Mark 3. O & B mark.

Mark 4. This is a rare mark used only for a few samples that were exhibited at the New Orleans Exposition in 1885.

Mark 5. Double mark. Some collectors called it a transitional mark, but we have strong reservations about this, as we could not find any literature to substantiate such an assertion.

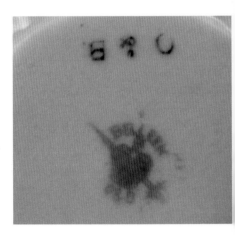

Mark 6. This is another double mark. O & B produced American Belleek for ten years and we could not find any literature to support that there was a transition at O & B in that period. Double mark items are more desirable by collectors.

Mark 7. Red crown mark. Note that the shapes of both the crown and sword are different from those of Mark 8.

Mark 8. Red crown mark. Note that the shapes of both the crown and sword are different from those of Mark 7.

Plates 180 and 181. Two wing-like
handled jar with lid, gilt-painted and
hand-painted with apple blossoms
and leaves on an ivory satin ground.
Mark 8, 4-3/4" x 5-1/2", $800-1,000.

Ott & Brewer items with color
decorations are highly desirable. A
similar jar with only gilded decoration,
$475-675.

Plates 182 and 183. Two handled round jar without lid, gilt-painted with flowers and leaves on front, and with a butterfly on back on an ivory satin ground. It has little round gold balls as feet. Small area of touch up to rim, Mark 8, 3-1/2" x 3-1/4", $450-650. Similar jar without butterfly, $275-375.

Plate 186. The back side of Plate 187.

Plate 184. Potpourri jar with a reticulated lid, hand-painted with gilded thistles on an ivory satin ground embossed floral pattern. Mark 8, 5" H, restored crack to lid, $650-750; without restoration $800-1,000. Note: someone may sell the jar without the lid as a vase.

Plate 185. Mini basket with applied branch handle; hand-painted with gilded flowers and leaves on both sides, and has a grid-like pattern as background. Rare item and more difficult to find than larger baskets. Mark 6, 3-1/2" H x 4-1/2" L, $600-700.

99

Plate 187. Gourd-shaped basket with free form scalloped rim and applied sponged gold branch handle and was hand-decorated with gilded thistles on an ivory satin ground. The asymmetrical slant rim of this vessel is a break away from the conventional style that was dominant at the times. These types of baskets usually have some sorts of damage but this one is mint. Mark 8, 8" H x 5-1/2", $1,750-2,500.

Plate 188. Ovoid vase with close-in rim, hand-painted with gilded daisies and leaves on an ivory satin ground. O & B vases are more difficult to find than pitchers. Mark 8, 6" H, $950-1,150.

Plate 189. Bread plate, hand-painted with gilded thistles and leaves on an embossed ivory satin ground. Mark 8, 6-1/2", $175-225.

Plate 190. Demitasse sugar bowl with piecrust-like wavy rim, hand-decorated with gilt-painted weeds and flowers on an ivory satin ground; unusual size. Mark 8, 1-1/2" H x 3", small nicks to rim, $150-200; mint $250-275.

Plate 191. Rare square footed tray with scalloped rim, hand-painted and signed by Walter Marsh with pink lilies and color leaves. O & B items signed by artists are almost never heard of (except this one), especially by noted artists. Square trays were among the first items produced by Ott & Brewer, and have been illustrated in many books of American ceramics in the nineteenth century. Without a square tray, many collectors consider a collection of O & B incomplete. Mark 8, 8-1/4", minimum $3,000.

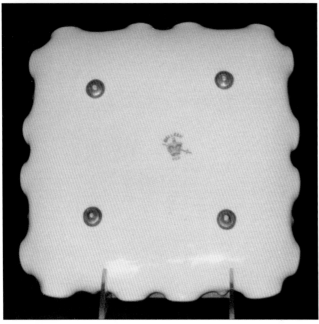

Plate 191a. The underside of the square tray showing 4 gilded feet.

Plate 192. Rare square tray (not footed) with scalloped rim, hand-painted with bucolic scene and fisherman with purple and gilded border. Ott and Brewer items with scenic decorations are among the rarest pieces ever made by the company. Items with birds and landscape background are more common, and some collectors consider them as game bird items. Like the plate signed by W. Marsh (Plate 191), this is the only scenic plate we have ever seen. Mark 1, 8-1/4", minimum $3,000.

Square tray with game birds, either with or without gilded feet, $1,100-1,250.

Plate 193. Square footed tray with scalloped rim, hand-decorated with colorful Parrot Tulips with gilded outlines on an ivory satin ground, a few small chips to edge. Mark 8, 8-1/4", $950-1,150; mint $1,100-1,250. Square with only gilt-painted decoration in same condition, $600-750 and $750-950 if mint.

Most of these square trays (also called plates) have small chips around their rims, which should not deter collectors from collecting them, although they will be discounted by 10-15%. Square trays are a must-have for serious collectors of O & B. These trays were highly regarded by many authors.

Plate 194. Lunch plate with scalloped rim, hand-painted with gold flowers and enameled green and pink leaves on an ivory satin ground. Like the square trays, these plates usually have small chips to their scalloped rims; this one is mint. Mark 1, 8-3/4", $500-600. Plates with only gilded decoration, $300-400, see Plate 315.

Plates 195 and 196. Eggshell bowl, decorated with gilt-painted flowers, leaves, and a butterfly on its back. Mark 8, 1-3/4" H x 3-1/2" D, $250-275; without butterfly $175-200.

Plate 197. Lunch plate with scalloped rim, hand-painted with colorful water lilies and a gold dragonfly over a pond with leaves and flowers on an ivory satin ground; unusual decoration. Mark 1, 8-3/4", $750-950.

Plates 198 and 199. Eggshell creamer, decorated with gilt-painted flowers, leaves, and a butterfly on its back. Mark 8, 2" H, $250-275; without butterfly $175-200.

Plate 200. Lunch plate, decorated with gilt-painted cherry blossoms and leaves. Mark 8, 8-3/4", $275-350.

Plate 201. Unusual sugar bowl with metal lid, hand-painted with colorful morning glory and gold leaves on a textured ground. Mark 1, 3-1/8", $325-375.

Plate 202. Eggshell sugar bowl with lid, hand-painted with cherry blossoms and leaves. The lids are so delicate and small that they usually do not survive. Mark 1, 3-1/2" H, $300-350.

Plate 203. Lunch plate with scalloped rim, hand-painted with colorful Dendrobium Orchid and leaves. Decorations with orchids are highly desirable. Mark 1, 8-1/2", $900-1,200.

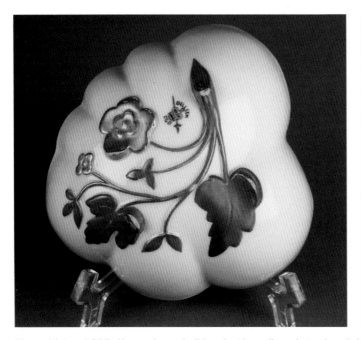

Plates 204 and 205. Unusual eggshell bowl with scalloped rim, hand-decorated with gilt-painted flowers and leaves inside, and embossed with gilded floral decoration on base. Mark 8, 2" H x 4-5/8" x 5", $425-525.

Plate 206. Small wafer tray with scalloped rim, hand-painted with colorful iris and leaves on an ivory satin ground. Iris decoration is highly desirable. Small chips to rim. Mark 1, 5", $275-375 each.

Plates 207 and 208. Unusual shape pitcher, and painted with blue and pink chrysanthemums in gilded outlines and gold leaves on satin ground. The rear part of this pitcher has an embossed shield-like pattern on a glazed ground with bend of stylish symbols on top. A rare find. Mark 8, 6-1/4" H, $1,000-1,200.

Plate 209. Small wafer tray with scalloped rim, hand-painted with pink flowers and leaves in two colors. The artwork on this small tray was in minute and exquisite detail. Small chips to rim. Mark 1, 4-3/4", $225-275.

Plate 211. Very rare shaker, hand-painted with red berries and leaves. Mark 1, 3", $200-300.

Plate 210. Lobed bowl, hand-painted with gilded flowers and leaves in three colors. The matte ground has a quilt-like embossed design. Mark 1, 2-3/4" x 4-1/4", $375-450.

Plate 212. Horn-shaped pitcher with bark base and applied tree-branch handle, hand-painted with pink and turquoise chrysanthemums in gilded outlines and gold leaves on satin ground. It has a complex pattern with time-consuming gilded outlines. Small restored chip to spout. Mark 8, 6-1/2" H, $750-950 or $1,100-1,300 if mint. Similar pitcher with only gilt-painted decoration, $800-1,000 if mint.

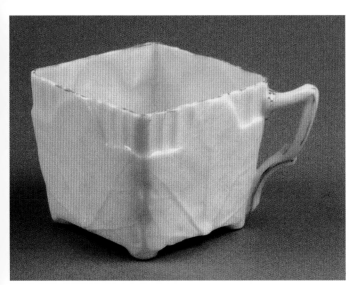

Plate 213. Eggshell creamer with maple leaves embossed on a shiny white ground and light lemon color inside. Mark 8, 1-3/4" H, $85-95.

Plate 214. Eggshell cup and saucer set, decorated with gilt-painted flowers and leaves. Mark 8, cup 2" H, saucer 5-3/8" D, $225-275 a set.

Plate 215. Teapot with tree bark base and branch handle. Decorated with gilt-painted flowers and leaves on a satin ground. This type of teapot is more difficult to find than the Tridacna pattern. Small factory imperfection inside lid. Mark 8, 5-1/2" H, $850-1,000.

Plate 216. Footed cup with unusual handle, missing saucer, hand-painted with pink enamel flowers and green leaves. It has a pink luster glaze inside. This cup was used for the New Orleans Exhibition in 1885. Mark 2, 2-3/4", $100-125.

Plate 217. Demitasse footed cup and saucer, hand-painted with purple and white enamel flowers and green leaves. This set was used for the New Orleans Exhibition in 1885. Mark 2 and 4, cup 2-3/4", saucer 5-1/4", $350-450 a set.

Plate 218. Demitasse eggshell cup and saucer, hand-decorated with gilt-painted flowers and leaves. Mark 8, cup 2" H, saucer 4-1/4" D, $250-275.

Plate 219. Demitasse eggshell cup and saucer, hand-decorated with red flowers and gilt-painted leaves. Mark 1, cup 1-3/4" H, saucer 4-3/4" D, $350-400 a set.

Plate 220. Demitasse eggshell cup and saucer, hand-decorated with gilt-painted thistles and leaves. Mark 8, cup 3" H, saucer 4-1/4" D, $250-275 a set.

Plate 221. Beautiful and fine cups and saucers, hand-decorated with gilded and beaded turquoise-enameled rim and gold ring handles; very thin. Mark 1, cup 2-3/8" H, saucer 5-1/2", $125-150 a set.

Plate 222. Two-handled eggshell bouillon cup and saucer, hand-decorated with gilt-painted thistles and leaves. Mark 6, cup 2-1/4" H, saucer 5-3/4", $325-375.

Plate 223. Eggshell cup and saucer with pink interior, hand-decorated with gilt-painted flowers and leaves and a butterfly on the back of the cup. Mark 8, cup 1-3/4" H, saucer 5-1/2" D, $300-350.

Plate 224. Butterfly of Plate 223.

Plate 226. Butterfly of Plate 225.

Plate 225. Eggshell cup and saucer hand-decorated with gilt-painted flowers and leaves and a butterfly on the back of the cup. Mark 8, cup 2" H, Mark 3, saucer 4-5/8" D, $275-325.

Plate 227. Eggshell cup and saucer hand-decorated with gilt-painted flowers and leaves and a butterfly on the back of the cup. Marks 1 & 4, cup 1-3/4" H, saucer 5-1/4" D, $275-325.

Plate 228. Butterfly of Plate 227.

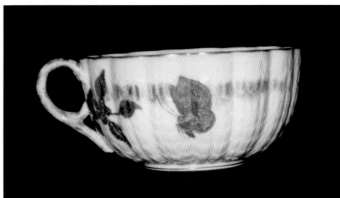

Plate 230. Butterfly of Plate 229.

Plate 229. Eggshell cup and saucer hand-decorated with gilt-painted flowers and leaves and a butterfly on the back of the cup. Mark 1, cup 2" H, Mark 8, saucer 5-1/2" D, $275-325.

Plate 231. Eggshell cup and saucer with pink interior. Cactus mold with applied cactus handles. Mark 8, cup 2" H, saucer 5-7/8" D, $300-350. Note that Plates 231 and 232 are different sizes but have the same price.

Plate 232. Eggshell cup and saucer with pink interior. Cactus mold with applied cactus handles. Mark 8, cup 1-1/2" H, saucer 4-7/8" D, $300-350 a set.

Plate 233. Leaf-shaped bowl and underplate with ivory exterior and pink interior. Minute wear to pink color. Mark 8 and Tiffany mark, bowl 5" D x 2" H, underplate 6 1/2", $400-450 a set.

Plates 234 to 239. Bowls with scalloped rim, hand-decorated with gilt-painted flower leaves, and a butterfly on an ivory satin ground. Mark 1 or 5, 2" H x 4-1/8", $250-275 each bowl.

Plates 240 to 241. Eggshell tea set, hand-decorated with gilt-painted flowers, leaves, and butterflies. Mark 8 for teapot (4-1/4" H with small fleck) and creamer (2 1/2" H); Mark 1 for sugar bowl (1-3/4" H), $1,250-1,500 a set.

Plate 242. Gourd-shaped pitcher with applied lotus leaves and branch handle, hand-painted with yellow lotus and gilded leaves on an ivory satin ground; restoration to two applied leaves and to handle. Ott and Brewer items with applied decoration usually have some sort of damages. Mint pieces are rare. Mark 8, 9-1/2" x 7-1/2", $1,750-2,000 or $2,500-3,000 if mint.

Plate 243. Bulbous pitcher with cactus handle and bamboo neck, hand-decorated
with gilt-painted daisies on an ivory satin ground; restoration to handle & spout.
Mark 6, 8-1/4" x 7-1/2", $1,100-1,300 or $1,300-1,500 if mint.

Plate 244. Pitcher with branch handle, hand-decorated with pink lilies and leaves on an ivory satin ground. Mark 8, 9-1/4" x 6-1/4", $2,250-2,750.

Plate 245. RARE Egg Server with Dolphin handle, gilt-painted with bamboo stalks. Mark 1, 5" x 7", $650-750.

Plate 246. Pitcher with branch handle and shell mold; hand-decorated with gilt-painted Cherry Blossoms and leaves on an ivory satin ground. Mark 8, 6-1/2" H, $700-850.

Plate 248. The back side of Plate 247.

Plate 247. Pitcher with applied branch handle, hand gilt-painted with wildflowers on an ivory satin ground. Mark 8, 10-1/2" x 5-1/2", $1,350-1,750.

Plate 249. Pitcher, embossed with ivy leaves & fruits on an ivory ground, brown handle and pink interior. Marked with "New Orleans Exposition 1885 Ott & Brewer Trenton NJ", Mark 4, 4-5/8" H, $250-300.

Plates 250 to 251. Very rare teapot with lots of applied branches on spout and lid, hand-decorated with blue & pink chrysanthemums and gilt-painted leaves on a white ground; repaired spout. Mark 8, 7" x 9-1/4", $2,000-2,500.

Plates 252 to 253. Four-part vase, hand-decorated with pink roses and gilt-painted leaves; small nicks to rim. Mark 8, 4-1/4" H, $375-425.

Chapter 4
Willets Manufacturing Company

In February of 1879, three brothers, Joseph, Daniel, and Edmund R. Willets, bought out the Excelsior Pottery built by William Young and Sons Company. The Youngs built a pottery in a four-acre site along the western bank of the Delaware and Raritan Canal near the Brunswick Turnpike around 1857. (Goldberg 1998, 14) It was acknowledged as the first effective white ware factory in Trenton (Potteries of Trenton Society, 6).

Although they were involved with the importation and sale of crockery wares in the New York City area, the Willets brothers had little experience in pottery making before this venture (Goldberg 1998, 16). In this new site, they divided their responsibilities clearly. Joseph was the general manager, Daniel took charge of the New York office, and Edmund concentrated on learning the manufacturing process. They were devout Quakers and brought their religious convictions into their business. Thus they set very strict rules for the workforce. One of those rules was to prohibit smoking while at work. The division of labor of the management team, the tight ship they ran, and the well-constructed physical plant they inherited all proved to be very effective. The company started with four kilns and, by 1882, had expanded to fourteen kilns and employed about 300 hands (Goldberg 1998, 16). At the beginning of their business, they produced a wide range of items such as sanitary earthenware, plumber's specialties, white and decorated pottery, electrical porcelain, opaque china, white granitewares and art porcelain.

Around 1884, William Bromely, Sr., after successfully helping the Ott & Brewer Co. make Belleek wares, went to help Willets do the same. As a result, Willets began producing Belleek wares around late 1884 or early 1885 (Gaston 1984). By putting a lot of time, money, and efforts into perfecting these art wares, they gradually shifted the emphasis from their more traditional products to the Belleek wares. New designs of Belleek were constantly put out. Another pioneer, Walter Scott Lenox, who once worked at Ott & Brewer, was hired to head their design department. During that period, many other competent artists were employed as well. Among them were Edward Stafford Challinor, Han John Nosek, Renelt, George Yarnold Houghton and Oliver Houghton, and Walter Marsh. (Robinson, 35-43) Their art wares were famous for their graceful and artistic styles, their delicate openwork handles, and their intricately modeled flowers. Their products included tea sets, enamel decorated plates, bouillon cups, vases, cabinet pieces, and picture frames, with many of them molded in shell or coral form (Reilly, 6). Eventually, Willets produced hundreds of products. Some of their forms and designs shown in their catalog in 1893 are seen in the last chapter of this book.

In less than ten years since they first made their white eggshell wares, Willets' American Belleek items were not only compared favorably with the industry leader Ott & Brewer, but they were also highly competitive with many European companies such as those in Dresden and Limoges in supplying white art porcelain to decorators (Barber 1893, 233). Unfortunately, the industry as a whole began to decline due to many factors, and by 1909 they had stopped making Belleek and ended their long period of about twenty-four years of producing American Belleek.

Marks for Willets Manufacturing Company

Although the company had a few marks, Willets basically used one snake mark in different colors to indicate its inventory system. The colors used were red, brown, black, green, and blue. Red, brown, and black were mainly used for factory decorated item; green was mainly for white ware; and blue was for Delftware. However, keep in mind that Willet did not have a strict quality control system, and we have seen beautiful factory decorated items with a green mark and poorly decorated items with brown marks. So we used the word "mainly" to describe the marks. For some eggshell items, the words EGGSHELL may also appear next to the snake mark. Except mark 1, which was used prior to the other marks, all marks were used from c. 1880 to 1904.

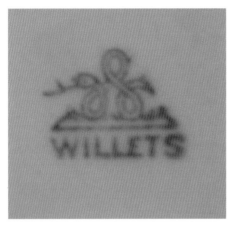

Mark 1. Light brown snake (or serpent) mark, also in other colors, without the word BELLEEK. This is a rather rarely used mark, and was believed to be the first mark used by Willets for its Belleek items.

Mark 2. Red or light brown (similar to color of Mark 1) snake mark mainly used for factory-decorated items.

Mark 3. Dark brown or black snake mark mainly used for factory-decorated items, but also on white wares.

Mark 4. Green snake mark mainly used for white wares sold to amateurs, but occasionally used for factory-decorated items.

Mark 5. Blue snake mark mainly used for its Delft items. Sometimes the word "Delft" also appeared next to the snake mark. Keep in mind that not all the items that were decorated in blue were Delft pieces as some amateur may use only blue paint to decorate the items.

Mark 6. Lion mark. This mark was used before Willets concentrated its business in producing belleek items. It appeared more on porcelain or stoneware than on belleek.

Plate 254. Covered Jar, factory hand-painted with pink hibiscus and
leaves, Willets product shape #6. Mark 2, 8" H, $450-550.

Plates 255. Covered Jar, factory or professionally hand-painted with an ermine clad Victorian woman on one side and a bouquet of flowers on another side; small nick to finial. Unmark but was identified as Willets' shape #6 like the one in Plate 254, 8" x 4-1/2", $500-600 or $700-800 if mint.

Plates 256. Same as Plate 255. Many Willets items were not marked like this covered jar. However, some of them can be identified with Willets' product shapes, and ideally together with their sizes. For example, this jar has the exact same shape and size of the jar in Plate 254, which was marked. Other unmarked examples are illustrated in Plates 257 to 261.

Plates 257 and 258. Cylindrical vase with three gilded
scrolled feet & scalloped rim, hand-painted with yellow
and pink roses and leaves on both sides; signed by
Marsh and dated 1909. Unmarked, 13-5/8", $1,500-
1,750.

Plates 259 and 260. Cylindrical vase with three gilded scrolled feet & scalloped rim, hand-painted with bouquets of violets and leaves on both sides; signed by Marsh and dated 1909, Mark 1, 14-1/8", $1,500-2,000.

Plate 261. Vase with pierced gold handles, hand-painted with pink tea roses by Walter Marsh; signed and dated 1909. Unmarked but shape #92 was identified, 8" x 6", $850-950.

Plate 262. Heart-shaped Tray, factory hand-decorated with holly leaves and berries. Mark 3, 5-1/2" x 5", $150-175.

Plate 263. Heart-shaped Tray, decorated with transfer-print portraits. Mark 2, 5-1/2" x 5", $95-120.

Plates 264 and 265. Large Chalice, hand-painted with raspberries and leaves on a shaded blue and pink ground, and applied garnet cabochons with gilded details; signed. Very rare to find American Belleek items with applied cabochons. Mark 2, 11" H, $1,500-2,000. Without cabochons, $1,000-1,200. Also see Plate 339.

Plate 266. Bowl with scalloped rim and two gilded handles, factory-decorated with garlands of flowers and leaves and gilded details. Mark 2, 3-1/2" x 6-1/4", $250-300.

Plate 268. Bowl with Gilded Accent. Shape #8. Mark 2, 1" H x 4" x 6", $65-85. Also see Plate 347.

Plate 267. Plate, hand-decorated with flowers and leaves on a soft pastel ground. Mark 2, 7-1/2", $125-150.

Plate 269. Covered Bouillon Cup, with factory hand-gilded decoration. Shape #162. Mark 2, cup 4-1/2" x 2-7/8", saucer 5-1/4", $325-375 a set.

Plate 270. Pitcher with unusual gilded handle, factory hand-painted with flowers and leaves. Shape #118. Mark 2, 4-3/4" H, $200-250.

Plate 271. Sugar bowl with lid, made before Willets fully markets its Belleek products, old Mark 6, 6-5/8" H, $65-75.

Chapter 5
Other Companies

History of Knowles, Taylor and Knowles

In 1854, two potters, Isaac W. Knowles and Isaac A. Harvey, started with a single kiln to make yellow ware in East Liverpool, Ohio. Gradually, they added Rockingham ware to their product line. When Harvey left the company, two other potters, John N. Taylor and Homer S. Knowles, joined the company in 1870. Two years later, they started making ironstone china. In 1888, Joseph Lee and Willis A. Knowles joined the company, and three years later they formed a corporation under the name of the Knowles, Taylor & Knowles Co. with a paid up capital of one million dollars. They prospered and grew, mainly because of the great demand in the trade of their superior quality hotel china. By 1893, they were operating thirty-five kilns in a ten-acre facility employing about 700 hands. (Barber 1893, 201)

Around 1887, Joshua Poole was hired from the Irish Belleek factory for his skill in making Belleek porcelain wares. (Schwartz 1969) As a result, a quantity of Belleek-like china wares were produced until a fire in November of 1889 destroyed their china works (Kearns, 7). Due to a more pressing demand for their staple goods, production of porcelain artwares took a back seat and the destroyed china works was not immediately rebuilt after the fire. Perhaps with the Chicago Exhibition in mind, they began to put more effort into putting out finer decorative artwares of a translucent and thin china body. In the 1893 Chicago Exhibition, their efforts were acknowledged when special attention was paid to their "Lotus" ware, a translucent bone china body ware with a soft, velvety glaze and decorated in dainty colors, or in jeweled and openwork effects. (Barber 1893, 204) "Lotus Ware" was different in composition from Irish Belleek. It was bone china and used calcined bones of animals in the clay body paste. The ware was pure white instead of having the orange tinge of porcelain made by other pottery working techniques during the same time period. Henry Schmidt, a renowned German decorator working for the company, was noted for his "squeeze-bag" design. William and George Morley had worked for K.T. & K. until around 1890. (Robinson, 42)

The economic situation in the US during the early 1890s led to decline in demand for expensive items like china wares. Knowles, Taylor & Knowles finally stopped making Lotus Wares around 1896. Lotus Ware enjoyed a short production life of only about five to six years. (Gaston 1984, 47)

American Art China Works

In 1891, Rittenhouse and Evans formed the American Art China Works (AACW) on Mulberry Street between St. Joe's and Breunig Avenues in Trenton. They were ambitious and decided to make fine quality porcelain ware. When comparing AACW's Belleek wares with those of its competitors, AACW's Belleek wares are slightly whiter in color. The company produced both decorated and undecorated fine examples of tableware and art wares. In January 1895 the company went out of business and liquidated all of its assets (Goldberg, 53).

Columbian Art Pottery

Columbian Art Pottery was founded in 1893 by W. T. Morris and F. R. Willmore. The company was named to honor the World's Columbian Exposition held in Chicago the same year. The company mark was composed of a shield with the owners' initials, so it was better known as Morris and Willmore. Both gentlemen were immigrants. Before coming to America, Morris had worked at the Irish Belleek Factory and the English Royal Worcester Works and Willmore had worked at the latter company. When in America, they had both worked for Ott & Brewer. They made opaque wares and Belleek-type wares. Souvenir and commemorative items, artistic tableware, and transfer-decorated mugs and tankards, which were touched up by hand, were also made. The company closed its doors around 1902 (Gaston 1984).

Coxon Belleek Pottery

Jonathan Coxon, who established the Ceramic Art Company with Walter Lenox in Trenton, was an influential man in the pottery industry. Many of his descendents were involved with major potteries in the country. Two of his sons, Frederick and Edward, established the Coxon Belleek Pottery in 1926 in Wooster, Ohio. They were well armed with the knowledge of making Belleek and produced very fine specimens. Their main line was dinnerware and was sold across the country. They decorated their wares with transfer, then hand fill-in, and touch-up.

Enameling and coin-gold designs were also common on their products. Due to the depression, high cost of production, and keen competition from the Morgan Belleek China Company, Coxon Belleek Pottery was forced to close in 1930 (Gaston 1984).

Morgan Belleek China Company

Morgan Belleek China Company was founded in 1923 in Canton, Ohio, under the name of Rea Company. It changed its name to Morgan Belleek China Company when William Morgan took over its production operations in 1924. Morgan had worked for the Lenox Company in Trenton and was well versed in Belleek making. The Belleek ware he put out was so fine that it competed successfully with the Lenox Belleek. Many of their dinnerware items were beautifully decorated with 24 karat gold trim and hand enameled designs. The company was doing so well that in 1929 The Irish Belleek Pottery Limited filed a suit against it to try to stop it from using the word Belleek to identify their products. The Irish company won the case and since then no other company could market their products as Belleek. The loss of this identity, plus competition from the Coxon Belleek Company, forced it to close in 1929 (Gaston 1984).

Marks for Other American Belleek Companies

We illustrated a few samples of American Belleek made by other companies in this chapter. These companies were in business for a very short period of time, and as we discussed in our preface, we give only a few examples.

Mark 1. Knowles, Taylor, and Knowles Lotus ware mark, 1891-1896. The company also used a simple letter mark of "K.T. & K/ CHINA" on its items.

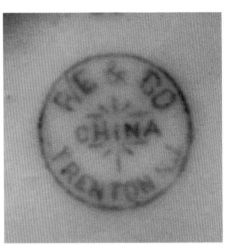

Mark 2. American Art China (Rittenhouse and Evans) or R. E. & Co., 1891-1895.

Mark 3. American Art China (Rittenhouse and Evans) or R. E. & Co., 1891-1895.

Mark 4. Columbian Art Company (Morris and Willmore), 1893-1902.

Mark 5. Morgan Belleek China Company, 1924-1929.

Mark 6. Coxon Belleek Pottery, 1926-1930.

Plate 302. Knowles Taylor and Knowles (KTK) Lotus Ware two-handle vase, hand-painted with flowers and leaves. Mark 1, 9" H, $750-950.

Plate 303. KTK Lotus Ware bowl with scalloped rim, hand-decorated with roses on a light green ground. Mark 1, 2-1/2" H x 5" D, $350-450.

Plate 304. KTK Lotus Ware bowl with scalloped rim (chips to rim) and hand decoration on embossed flowers and leaves. Mark 1, 4" x 5", $100-125 or $400-500 if mint.

Plate 305. KTK Lotus Ware pitcher, hand-decorated with gilded floral designs and fishnet; restored spout. Mark 1, 5-1/4" H, $325-375 or $650-750 if mint.

Plate 306. Columbian Art Pottery eggshell cup and saucer in pink. Mark 4, cup 1-1/2", saucer 4-5/8", $175-250 a set.

Plate 307. Rittenhouse and Evans (R.E./American Art China) pitcher, hand-decorated with gilded flowers; small nick to spout. Mark 2, 4" x 4-1/4", $250-350.

Plate 308. Rittenhouse and Evans (R.E./American Art China) demitasse cup and saucer, hand-painted with roses on a pink ground. Mark 3, cup 3-1/8", saucer 5", $275-350.

Plate 309. Columbia Art Pottery footed cup, hand-decorated with pink flowers. Mark 4, 3", $125-150.

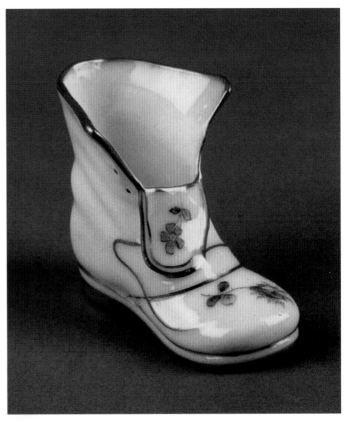

Plate 310. Rare, miniature shoe, hand-painted with small flower, unmarked but attributed to Columbian Art Pottery. 1-7/8" H, $300-400. An identical but undecorated white shoe was sold on the internet in October 2002 for over $250.

Plate 311. Morgan Belleek dinner plate, extensively hand-decorated with enamels on printed transfer fruit basket with gold-etched rim; short scratch to blue area. Mark 5, 10-1/2", $300-400. Rare item.

Plate 312. Coxon dinner plate, decorated with transfer-print flowers, wears to inner gold ring. Mark 6, 10-1/2", $125-150.

Plate 313. Cup and saucer, decorated with transfer-print flowers. This set of cup and saucer shows how keen competition was among the companies. Cup was made by Morgan while saucer was produced by Coxon. They both used the exact same print to decorate their products. Mark 5 for cup and Mark 6 for saucer, cup 2-3/4", saucer 5-3/4", $75-100 a set.

Selected Items of American Belleek Sold Recently with Actual Selling Prices

Plate 314. O & B plate, 8-3/8", $300.

Plate 315. O & B plate, 8-3/8", several chips to rim, $300.

Plate 316. O & B plate, 9", $300.

Plate 317. O & B dish, 4-1/2", $75.

Plate 318. O & B square tray, 5-1/8", $400.

Plate 319. O & B plate, 6-1/2", $60.

Plate 320. O & B creamer, 2-1/8", $80.

Plate 321. O & B honey pot with restored hairlines, 5" H x 4-3/4", $1,100.

157

Plate 322. O & B pitcher, 4-5/8", $150.

Plate 323. O & B pitcher, 4-5/8", $450.

Plate 324. O & B cup and saucer, cup 2-1/8" H, saucer 4-7/8", $225.

Plates 325 and 326. O & B sugar bowl, no butterfly, 4-1/8", $185.

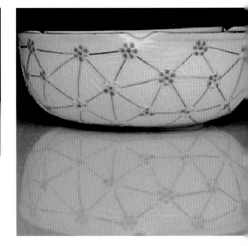

Plate 327. O & B bowl, 2-3/4" H x 8" D, $185.

Plates 328 and 329. Tea set, teapot with restoration to lid, 5" H; sugar, 3-1/2" H; and creamer, 2-3/4", $1,100 a set.

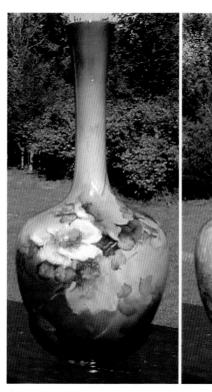

Plate 330. Willets tall vase, spider to base, 14", $400.

Plates 331 and 332. Ceramic Art Company (CAC) vase, 12-1/2", $800.

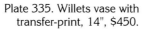

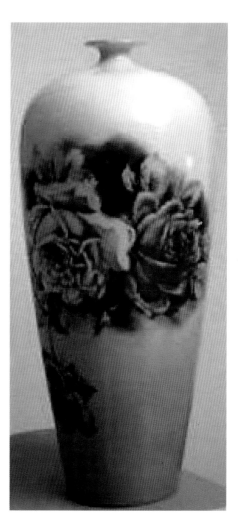

Plate 333. CAC pitcher, 3-3/4", $185.

Plate 334. CAC sugar bowl, 4-1/2", $95.

Plate 335. Willets vase with transfer-print, 14", $450.

Plate 338. Willets mug, 6", $265.

Plate 336. Willets tankard, 14-1/2", hairline to body, $225.

Plate 337. National Art China mug with transfer-print, 6", $110. Rare.

Plate 339. Willets chalice, 11-1/2", $1,600.

Plate 340. Willets mug, 6", $110.

Plate 341. Lenox mug, 6", $65.

Plate 342. O & B bouillon cup (2-1/2" H) and saucer (6" D), $350.

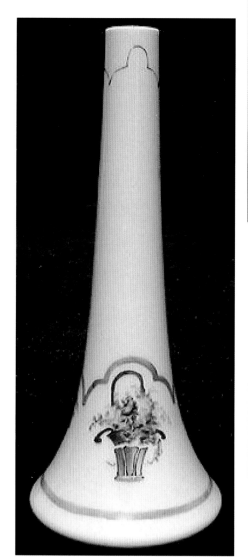

Plate 345. CAC bud vase, 8", $60.

Plates 343 and 344. CAC mug, 5-1/2", similar to the mug in Plates 155 and 156 and by the same artist. $250.

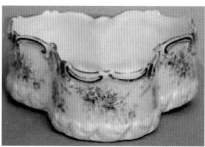

Plate 346. CAC bowl, 1-5/8" H x 4-5/8", $150.

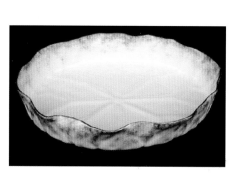

Plate 347. Willets bowl, 1-1/4" H x 6", similar to Plate 268, $95.

Selected Recent Paintings of Loman Eng

Among the artists who worked for Lenox and other American Belleek companies, Han John Nosek and Walter Marsh are Loman Eng's favorites. Loman's floral paintings are more in line with Walter Marsh than with the Morleys although he also enjoys works by them. Like Walter Marsh, Loman uses bolder strokes and brighter colors to express his passions for flowers and birds (Figure 3). Loman's portrait paintings are similar in forms and execution to Nosek's works, especially those that were painted with classical European techniques in tremendous details. Loman's black and white oil portrait paintings with color surroundings and background are particularly popular among art collectors (Figures 4 and 7). Loman also does excellent charcoal portraits (Figures 5 and 6). Denise Richer, an art and antiques writer, commented on Loman's portraits in her recent article as "*breathtaking*" and "*he can express color in black and white—he gets the mood…they seem almost living, capturing emotion, mood, and attitude in black-and-white charcoal form.*" (*Northeast Journal of Antiques and Arts*, November 2002)

Figure 3. "A Tale of Two Worlds" by Loman Eng, oil on canvas board, 20" x 30".

Figure 4. "Bringing You Good News" by Loman Eng, oil on canvas, 18" x 24".

Figure 5. "Debut" by Loman Eng, charcoal on paper, 18" x 24".

Figure 6. "Coy" by Loman Eng, charcoal on paper, 18" x 24".

Figure 7. "Wind Whisperer" by Loman Eng, oil on canvas, 18" x 24".

163

Willets Catalog and
Price List of 1893

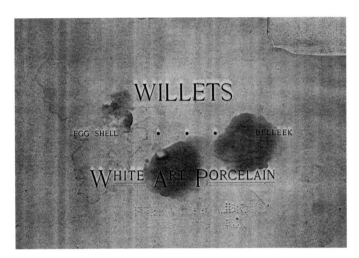

WILLETS

EGG SHELL . . . . . BELLEEK

WHITE ART PORCELAIN

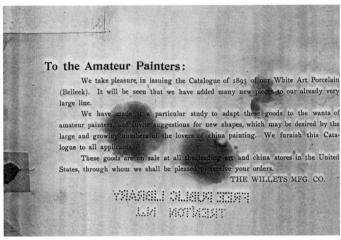

To the Amateur Painters:

We take pleasure in issuing the Catalogue of 1893 of our White Art Porcelain (Belleek). It will be seen that we have added many new pieces to our already very large line.

We have made it a particular study to adapt these goods to the wants of amateur painters, and invite suggestions for new shapes, which may be desired by the large and growing numbers of the lovers of china painting. We furnish this Catalogue to all applicants.

These goods are on sale at all the leading art and china stores in the United States, through whom we shall be pleased to receive your orders.

THE WILLETS MFG. CO.

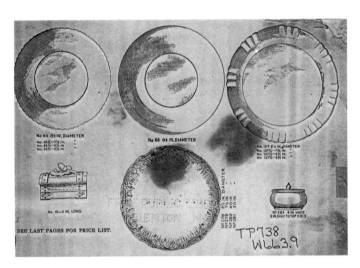

SEE LAST PAGES FOR PRICE LIST.

SEE LAST PAGES FOR PRICE LIST.

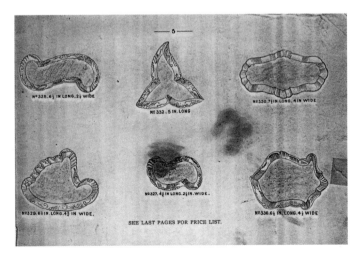

SEE LAST PAGES FOR PRICE LIST.

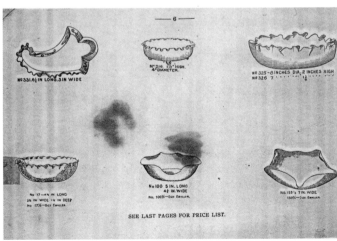

SEE LAST PAGES FOR PRICE LIST.

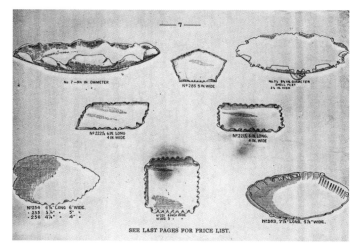

— 7 —

No. 7—9 IN. DIAMETER

No. 285 5 IN. WIDE

No. 73, 9½ IN. DIAMETER
SHELL FEET
2½ IN. HIGH

No. 222½, 6 IN. LONG,
4 IN. WIDE.

No. 221½, 6 IN. LONG,
4 IN. WIDE.

No. 254 6¼ IN. LONG 6 IN. WIDE.
- 255 5¾ "   5".
- 256 4¾ "   4".

No. 221 6 IN. HIGH WIDE.
- 202 5 "

No. 263, 7½ IN. LONG, 5½ IN. WIDE.

SEE LAST PAGES FOR PRICE LIST.

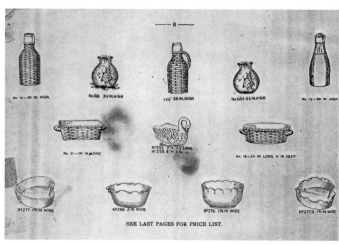

— 8 —

No. 14—1½ IN. HIGH

No. 68 2½ IN. HIGH

11½ 3½ IN. HIGH

No. 684 2½ IN. HIGH

No. 15—3½ IN. HIGH

No. 202 2½ IN. LONG
No. 253 4½ IN. ½

No. 21—7½ IN. LONG

No. 18—3½ IN. LONG, 4 IN. DEEP

No. 277 1½ IN. WIDE

No. 286 2 IN. WIDE

No. 276 1½ IN. WIDE

No. 277½ 1½ IN. WIDE

SEE LAST PAGES FOR PRICE LIST.

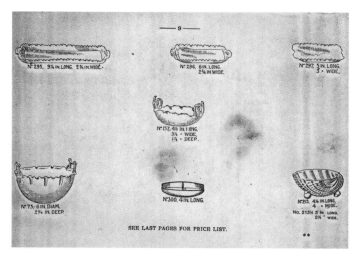

— 9 —

No. 295, 9¾ IN. LONG, 2¾ IN. WIDE.

No. 296, 6 IN. LONG,
2¾ IN. WIDE.

No. 297, 5 IN. LONG,
3 " WIDE.

No. 157, 4½ IN. LONG,
3¼ " WIDE,
1¼ " DEEP.

No. 73, 6 IN. DIAM.
2¾ IN. DEEP.

No. 300, 4 IN. LONG.

No. 213, 4½ IN. LONG,
4 " WIDE.
No. 213½, 3 IN. LONG,
2½ "

SEE LAST PAGES FOR PRICE LIST.

**

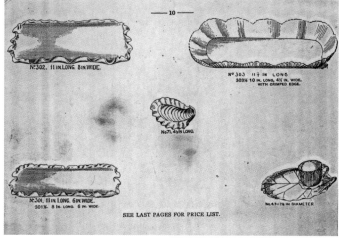

— 10 —

No. 302, 11 IN. LONG, 8 IN. WIDE.

No. 303 11½ IN. LONG
303½ 10 IN. LONG, 4½ IN. WIDE,
WITH CRIMPED EDGE.

No. 71, 4½ IN. LONG.

No. 301, 11 IN. LONG, 6 IN. WIDE.
301½ 8 IN. LONG, 6 IN. WIDE.

No. 4?—7½ IN. DIAMETER

SEE LAST PAGES FOR PRICE LIST.

— 11 —

No. 241 7 IN. HIGH,
5¼ IN. DIAMETER.

No. 173 8 IN. HIGH,
8 " WIDE.

No. 230 6 IN. HIGH. 5 IN. DIAMETER.

No. 190 6 IN. DIAMETER

No. 38 6 IN. HIGH
5 IN. DIAMETER

SEE LAST PAGES FOR PRICE LIST.

— 12 —

No. 234 3½ IN. HIGH.

No. 233 3¾ IN. HIGH.

No. 232 4¾ IN. HIGH.

No. 169 5 IN. HIGH.

No. 170 4½ IN. HIGH.

No. 171 2½ IN. HIGH.

SEE LAST PAGES FOR PRICE LIST.

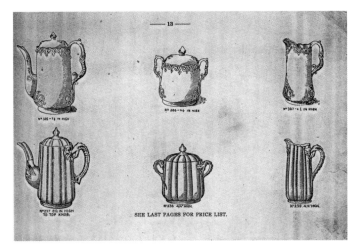

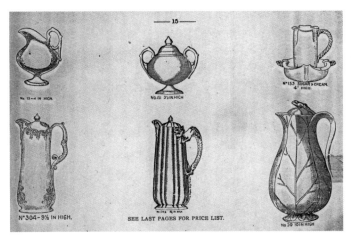

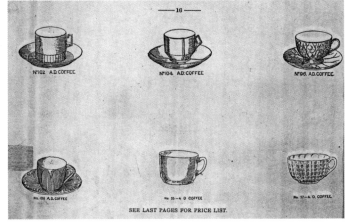

SEE LAST PAGES FOR PRICE LIST.

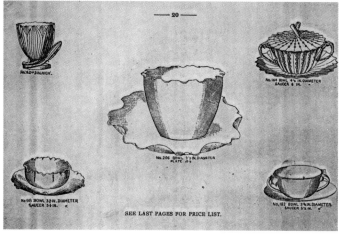

SEE LAST PAGES FOR PRICE LIST.

SEE LAST PAGES FOR PRICE LIST.

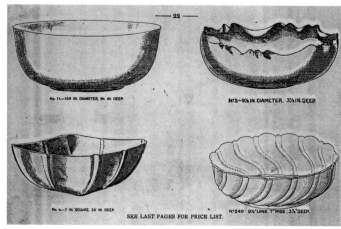

SEE LAST PAGES FOR PRICE LIST.

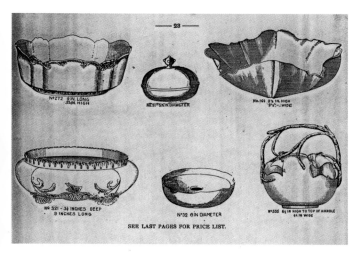

SEE LAST PAGES FOR PRICE LIST.

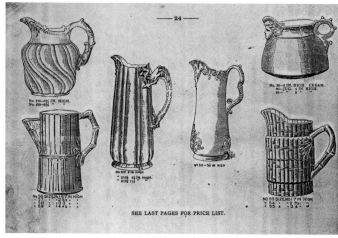

SEE LAST PAGES FOR PRICE LIST.

— 25 —

No.177 5½ IN. HIGH

No.101, 5 IN. HIGH
119, Same, only one dent in each side.
141, Same, only four dents in each side.
142, Same, only covered with dents.

No. 63, 10 IN. HIGH.

SEE LAST PAGES FOR PRICE LIST.

No.145 8½ IN. HIGH

No.118 8 IN. DIAMETER
5 IN. HIGH

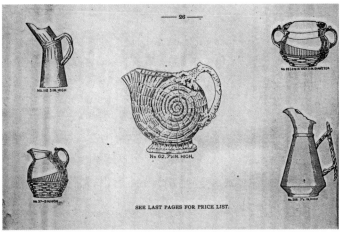

— 26 —

No.112 5 IN. HIGH

No.37–3 IN. HIGH

No. 62, 7½ IN. HIGH.

SEE LAST PAGES FOR PRICE LIST.

No.293 8 IN. HIGH 3 IN. DIAMETER

No.288. 7½ IN. HIGH

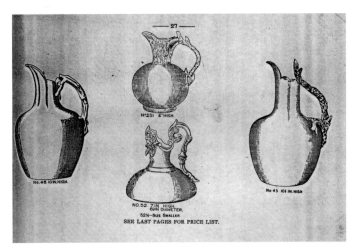

— 27 —

No. 46, 10 IN. HIGH.

Nº 231 6" HIGH

NO.52 7 IN. HIGH
6 IN DIAMETER.
52N–SIZE SMALLER

Nº 294

No 45 10½ IN. HIGH

SEE LAST PAGES FOR PRICE LIST.

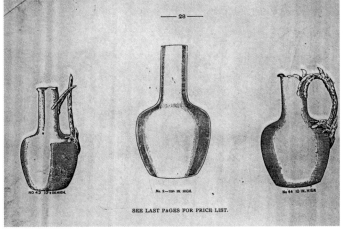

— 28 —

No 43 10½ IN. HIGH.

No. 9 –10½ IN. HIGH.

No. 44 10 IN. HIGH

SEE LAST PAGES FOR PRICE LIST.

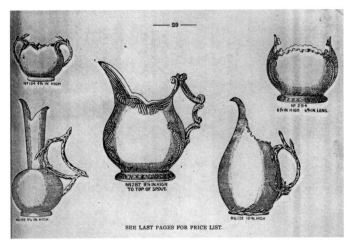

— 29 —

Nº 134 4½ IN. HIGH

Nº 294
6½ IN HIGH 6½ IN LONG.

No.159 9½ IN. HIGH

Nº287 9¾ IN. HIGH
TO TOP OF SPOUT.

No.129 10 IN. HIGH

SEE LAST PAGES FOR PRICE LIST.

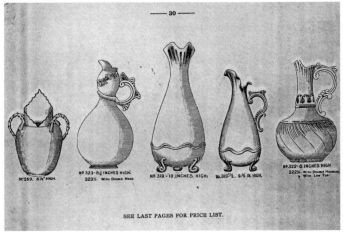

— 30 —

Nº269. 8½ IN. HIGH.

Nº 323–8¾ INCHES HIGH.
323½. WITH DOUBLE HAND.

Nº 319.–10. INCHES. HIGH.

No.319½. 8½ IN. HIGH.

Nº322–8 INCHES HIGH
322½. WITH DOUBLE HANDLES
& WITH LOW TOP.

SEE LAST PAGES FOR PRICE LIST.

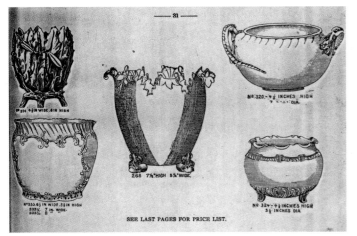

— 31 —

Nº 334 4½ IN WIDE. 6 IN HIGH

No. 320.-4½ INCHES HIGH
7½ IN. DIA.

2 68 7¾ HIGH 5¾ WIDE.

Nº 333 6½ IN WIDE. 5½ IN HIGH
333½ 7 IN. WIDE.
333½ 8 "

No. 329- 4½ INCHES HIGH
5¼ INCHES DIA

SEE LAST PAGES FOR PRICE LIST.

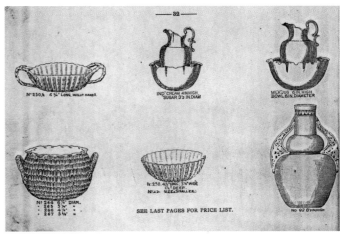

— 32 —

Nº 250 A 6¾" LONG. INCLUT HANDS.

IND' CREAM 4 IN HIGH
SUGAR 3½ IN. DIAM

MILK JUG 6 IN HIGH
BOWL 8 IN. DIAMETER

Nº 264 6¼" DIAM.
" 265 5¾"
" 266 5"
" 267 3¾"

Nº 250. 4½ LONG 3¾ WIDE
1¼ DEEP.
Nº 251 SIZE SMALLER.

No 92 8 IN HIGH

SEE LAST PAGES FOR PRICE LIST.

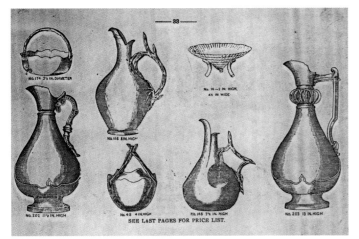

— 33 —

No. 174 3½ IN. DIAMETER

No. 166 8 IN. HIGH

Nº 16 — 2 IN. HIGH.
4½ IN. WIDE.

No. 202 11½ IN. HIGH

No. 48 4 IN HIGH

No. 148 7½ IN. HIGH

No. 203 13 IN. HIGH.

SEE LAST PAGES FOR PRICE LIST.

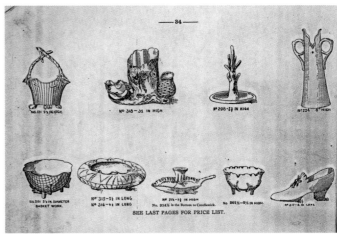

— 34 —

Nº 121 5½ IN. HIGH.

NO. 318 — 3½ IN HIGH

Nº 298 — 1½ IN HIGH

Nº 224 6" HIGH

No. 201 3½ IN. DIAMETER
BASKET WORK.

Nº 315 — 5½ IN LONG
No. 316 — 4½ IN LONG

No. 314½ IN the Bottom to Candlestick.
Nº 314½ — 1½ IN HIGH

No 201½ — 2½ IN HIGH.

Nº 317 — 6 IN LONG

SEE LAST PAGES FOR PRICE LIST.

— 35 —

Nº 290 4 IN. HIGH
2¾ IN. WIDE.

Nº 191 6" HIGH.
Nº 191A 4¾" HIGH.

Nº 291 3½ IN. WIDE
3 IN. HIGH

No 70 2½ IN HIGH

No 97 3½ IN. HIGH

No. 158 5½ WIDE

Nº 229 4" HIGH.

SEE LAST PAGES FOR PRICE LIST.

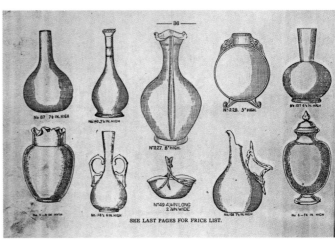

— 36 —

No 87 7¼ IN. HIGH

No 160 7½ IN. HIGH

Nº 227. 8" HIGH.

Nº 228. 5" HIGH.

No 137 6½ IN HIGH

No 1 — 8 IN HIGH

No 38½ 6 IN HIGH

Nº 149 4¾ IN LONG
2 IN WIDE

No 158 7½ IN HIGH

No 6 — 7¾ IN HIGH

SEE LAST PAGES FOR PRICE LIST.